THE SPIRIT OF CHRISTMAS

CREATIVE HOLIDAY IDEAS
BOOK NINETEEN

Christmas … it's an enchanting season when excitement fills the air and each friendly face takes on a cordial glow. To help you make it a joyful occasion, we filled this book with a host of decorating ideas — from retro to regal — that will transform your home into a glorious setting for Yuletide festivities. You'll find generous offerings of gifts and goodies to delight loved ones, as well as dozens of delectable menus for your holiday get-togethers. Throughout this time of merry memory-making, may your home … and your heart … be filled with the true spirit of the season.

LEISURE ARTS, INC.
Little Rock, Arkansas

THE SPIRIT OF CHRISTMAS

BOOK NINETEEN

EDITORIAL STAFF
Vice President and Editor-in-Chief: Sandra Graham Case
Executive Director of Publications: Cheryl Nodine Gunnells
Senior Director of Publications: Susan White Sullivan
Director of Designer Relations: Debra Nettles
Publications Director: Kristine Anderson Mertes
Senior Design Director: Cyndi Hansen
Special Projects Director: Susan Frantz Wiles
Director of Retail Marketing: Stephen Wilson
Art Operations Director: Jeff Curtis

OXMOOR HOUSE
Editor-in-Chief: Nancy Fitzpatrick Wyatt
Executive Editor: Susan Carlisle Payne
Foods Editor: McCharen Pratt
Senior Photographer: Jim Bathie
Photographer: Brit Huckabay
Contributing Photographer: John O'Hagan
Senior Photography Stylist: Kaye Clark
Photography Stylist: Amy Wilson
Test Kitchens Director: Elizabeth Tyler Luckett
Test Kitchens Assistant Director and Recipe Coordinator:
 Julie Christopher
Test Kitchens Staff: Kristi Carter, Nicole L. Faber,
 Kathleen Royal Phillips, Elise Weiss, and Kelley Self Wilton

TECHNICAL
Technical Editor: Leslie Schick Gorrell
Technical Writers: Shawnna Bowles and Jennifer S. Hutchings
Technical Associates: Sarah J. Green, Cathy Hardy,
 and Lois J. Long
Associate Foods Editor and Technical Writer:
 Laura Siar Holyfield

DESIGN
Design Manager: Diana Sanders Cates
Designers: Cherece Athy, Tonya Bradford Bates,
 Polly Tullis Browning, Peggy Elliott Cunningham, Kim Kern,
 Anne Pulliam Stocks, Linda Diehl Tiano, Lori Wenger,
 and Becky Werle

ART
Art Publications Director: Rhonda Shelby
Art Imaging Director: Mark Hawkins
Art Category Manager: Lora Puls
Lead Graphic Artist: Dayle Carozza
Graphic Artists: Autumn Hall, Andrea Hazlewood,
 Stephanie Stephens, Dana Vaughn, and Elaine Wheat
Imaging Technician: Mark R. Potter
Photographer: Lloyd Litsey
Photography Stylists: Cassie Francioni and Karen Smart Hall
Publishing Systems Administrator: Becky Riddle
Publishing Systems Assistants: Clint Hanson, Josh Hyatt,
 and John Rose

BUSINESS STAFF
Chief Operating Officer: Tom Siebenmorgen
Director of Corporate Planning and Development:
 Laticia Mull Dittrich
Vice President, Sales and Marketing: Pam Stebbins
Director of Sales and Services: Margaret Reinold
Vice President, Operations: Jim Dittrich
Comptroller, Operations: Rob Thieme
Retail Customer Service Manager: Stan Raynor
Print Production Manager: Fred F. Pruss

"... and it was always said of him, that he knew how to keep Christmas well, if any man alive possessed the knowledge. May that be truly said of us, and all of us!"
— From *A Christmas Carol* by Charles Dickens

Library of Congress Catalog Card Number 98-65188
Hardcover ISBN 1-57486-362-2
Softcover ISBN 1-57486-363-0

10 9 8 7 6 5 4 3 2 1

CONTENTS

The *Sights* of Christmas

The *Sights* of Christmas continued

The *Sharing* of Christmas

The *Tastes* of Christmas

The Sights

# of Christmas

Gaze into the eyes of every believer, both young and old alike, and you'll see it ... it's the wonder of Christmas! You can behold Yuletide's beauty everywhere — from stockings hung by the chimney with care to tables spread with holiday fare. Whether you prefer your seasonal décor to have royal splendor, whimsical touches, or something in between, we can help you create a sensational setting in which to make lasting memories. So may your heart be light as you take in the sights of Christmas!

Classic Cocoa & Cream

Your dinner guests will drink in the beauty of this richly decorated dining room. The botanical theme of magnolias and pears complements the warm cocoa and cream tones.

Lend your room a look of personalized elegance with Monogrammed Chair Back Covers. A striped Table Drape lays the foundation for a distinguished Tablescape and place settings that include a beribboned Dinner Napkin and a Pear Place Card Holder. Let Chandelier Lamp Shades cast a soft radiance over your holiday party.

Serve up a feast for the eyes and the taste buds! A stunning Bronze Urn Centerpiece *(above)* will make a dramatic arrangement for the holiday meal, which begins with tantalizing appetizers and a hearty soup. Rosemary Pork Tenderloin *(left)* with cranberry chutney is the highlight of the main course. Scalloped Potatoes and asparagus with Zesty Hollandaise Sauce are the rich and savory side dishes.

The Magnolia Leaf Wreath draws all eyes to a buffet sideboard. There, Easy Perfect Chocolate Cake, with its delectable layers, will have guests hinting for second servings.

Instructions and recipes for Classic Cocoa & Cream begin on page 122.

Olde World RADIANCE

Give your room Olde World radiance by wrapping it in rich color and texture. The fleur-de-lis symbol — traditionally used to represent French royalty and said to signify perfection, light, and life — highlights many of the accessories to add the crowning touch.

Gracing a mantel or sideboard, a set of **Lustrous Candlesticks** with **Embellished Candles** will make the season bright. The candles feature beautiful beaded fleur-de-lis designs, which are created with beads and sequin pins.

Pinecones are Mother Nature's tree trims and are ideal for decorating your own holiday evergreen. Embellished with paint and microbeads, these **Mossy Pinecone Ornaments** *(above, left)* are naturally appealing. A plain glass ball is easily transformed into a **Fleur-de-lis Ornament** *(above, right)* by adding a microbead pattern and highlighting it with gold embossing powder. Purchased accessories can become custom showpieces when enhanced with handmade touches. Striking fleur-de-lis motifs look noble on an **Embellished Throw** *(right)* and a coordinating **Boxed Pillow**. Sparkling beaded trim is a luxurious finish for a **Tufted Throw Pillow**.

Instructions for Olde World Radiance *begin on page 128.*

Reflecting the true reason for the season, this mesmerizing Madonna and Child Painting (*above*) will set hearts aglow. The artwork is framed by a pair of resplendent **Bronze Urn Arrangements**. A beaded Table Scarf, fashioned from a wool jacquard throw, is topped with more greenery, an assortment of ornaments, and **Lustrous Candlesticks** with Embellished Candles. Our **Cone-Shaped Stocking** (*left*) is an elegant alternative to the traditional Christmas stocking. The cuff repeats the jacquard motif, while a tassel adds a touch of whimsy.

RETRO
noel

Take a step back in time and capture the magic of Christmas past with these retro decorations. In colors as soft as memories, the vintage-look accessories will fill your home with glamour and glitz to make your holidays sparkle!

Create an eye-catching Vellum Mobile (*above, left*) with retro-print vellum paper. Shed light on the festivities with a trio of Glass Candleholders (*above, right*). Shimmering on a silver tree (*right*) are Vellum Ornaments, Painted Star Ornaments, Painted Glass Balls, and Retro Papier-Mâché Ornaments. Funky vellum and sticker-accented Ribbon Garland winds its way through the branches. And patchwork couldn't be simpler than on a beaded Square Tree Skirt.

Instructions for Retro Noel begin on page 131.

Mirrored Stars (*above*) serve as decorative reminders that the holiday season is the ideal time for reflection. These Retro Stockings are pretty in pink! The cuffs are accented with fabric squares to carry the nostalgic theme from the tree to the hearth. Painted in relaxing pastels and filled with artificial snow and pink beaded picks, the Serenity Vase (*left*) will bring quiet splendor to the mantel, a coffee table, or an end table.

merry & BRIGHT

Make all your holiday gatherings merry and bright by decorating your home with these jolly accessories! Providing a splash of color and a dash of fun, the whimsical creations are sure to get everyone in the Christmas spirit.

Delightfully different, this tablescape is so cheery you'll want to extend its use beyond the Christmas season. An easy-to-fashion Felt Table Runner is dressed up with colorful felt circles, rickrack, and pom-pom fringe. A merry mixture of Painted Wooden Candlesticks lends a bright touch while serving as a unique centerpiece. The star of each place setting is definitely the Elf! Armature wire gives these little fellows their shape and also makes them bendable, so they can hang from a glass, sit on a plate, or be positioned wherever you want them.

Instructions for Merry & Bright begin on page 134.

These **Felt Stockings** (*above*) will be hung by the chimney with cheer! Accented with an assortment of felt shapes and playful pom-poms, the fanciful elf boots will liven up your Yuletide mantel. Welcome guests into your home with the soft, inviting glow of these lighthearted Luminaries (*right*). Hand paint glass jars with stripes and dots to coordinate with your other jovial decorations.

The striking combination of bright hues and bold lines makes this Painted Wall Hanging (*above*) an eye-catching conversation piece. Fashioned from canvas, the artwork features a fun-to-form Christmas tree as its focal point. **Painted Wooden Candlesticks** (*left*), like those used on the table, are situated among greenery to give the mantel a warm ambience.

Instructions for Merry & Bright begin on page 134.

A trio of happy-go-lucky Elves encircles this Elf Wreath (left) to create a welcoming accent. Embellished with garlands of beads and suspended by a rickrack hanger, the wreath will add charm and character to your home. Deliver holiday cheer by filling our clever Felt Stockings (below) with gaily wrapped presents.

Personalize your holiday evergreen with ornaments you've made yourself. These vibrant tree trims (opposite) — **Felt Ornaments**, Bump Chenille Stars, **Elves**, **Papier-Mâché Ornaments**, and Wooden Top Ornaments — are so fun to create, the whole family will want to join you. And the time spent together will make the season even more special!

Instructions for Merry & Bright begin on page 134.

Winter Green

Arrayed in a tone-on-tone color palette, this room is the epitome of refreshing elegance. To give your Yuletide decorating a new look, simply make these magical accessories in lighter, brighter tints of a traditional Christmas color — green.

A beribboned white Christmas tree combines style with whimsy when Pom-Pom Garland and **Knit Garland** add a handmade touch.

Made from glass ornaments in a range of sizes and shades, the ornate Square Ornament Wreath (*opposite*) is a masterpiece. Dress the mantel in seasonal splendor by lining it with **Wrapped Packages**, then finish with a set of Knit Cuff Stockings to add fashionable flair. Create a striking tree by trimming it with a showcase of bright adornments (*right, top to bottom*) — Bead-Wrapped Ornaments, Flocked Ornaments with loops, **Gift Box Ornaments**, Flocked Ornaments with swirls, and Painted Ornaments. With its fun, furry knit edging, this Harlequin Tree Skirt (*below*) is an ideal complement to the tree.

Instructions for Winter Green begin on page 139.

These **Frame Place Card Holders** are miniature works of art. The tiny, beribboned wooden frames will make it easy for guests to find their seats. Featuring a lime green base with darker green polka dots, the Painted Wine Glasses coordinate beautifully with the rest of the table.

Instructions for Winter Green begin on page 139.

You'll be entertaining in grand style when you deck your dining room in an eye-pleasing palette of green. The Ribbon Centerpiece is sophisticated, yet easy to make. Simply tie lengths of ribbon around candles and string beads onto craft wire, then arrange in a free-flowing design. Embellished with a gift box pattern, the Painted Chargers remind us that holiday meals are presents to be appreciated, too.

When hung above the dining table, this Suspended Wreath serves as an eye-catching faux chandelier. Fabric, ribbons, and beaded wire garland are wrapped around a circular foam wreath, then a multitude of baubles are hung from the wreath using varying lengths and colors of ribbon.

It's a snap to restyle an understated table covering with an Ornamental Table Décor! At each corner of the table, simply gather the tablecloth, secure with rubber bands, and then tie on a ribbon bow. Wire together a trio of ornaments and wrap the wire around the gathered corner. Voilà! You've invested a little bit of time and received a big decorative dividend!

Instructions for Winter Green begin on page 139.

Mesmerize holiday visitors with a Lighted Stained Glass Panel. The various green hues of the glass pieces echo the room's tone-on-tone theme. Ideal for illuminating a sideboard or buffet table, the radiant treasure is a beauty to behold and fun to make. The panel is adhered to a vase, which is then filled with sand and a candle or Christmas lights.

A little candlelight can quickly change a room from cold to cozy. These Bead-Wrapped Candles are both bright and beautiful — you may decide to enjoy them long past the holiday season.

yuletide Fiesta

Turn your holiday celebrations into a fiesta with these south-of-the-border-inspired decorations! The festive blend of accents will spice up your kitchen and make serving up "season-ed" greetings even more fun.

Wish your family and friends glad tidings on a clever **Chalkboard Plate** (*above*) featuring a painted wooden disk in the center. A perky **Tea Towel Table Runner** (*right*) will dress up your table. Add festive **Napkins**, which are trimmed in rickrack and buttons, and finish with beaded, fruit-topped **Napkin Rings**. Continue the very merry mood by creating a **Yuletide Wreath** (*shown on page 37*) to hang in a window.

Looking for a unique tree stand? Use a ceramic pitcher! For a fun alternative to purchased garland, wind simple-to-make **Loop Garland** among the branches. Season the tree with a mixture of handmade ornaments — Matchstick Ornaments, **Fruit Ornaments**, and **Pot Holder Cones**. Finish your trimming by adding some faux Hens and Chicks and small stoneware-inspired ornaments.

You'll love this enlightening Fiesta Lamp! A nostalgic pitcher transforms easily into a luminous showpiece. Accentuate the lampshade with tea towels and rickrack to complete the look.

Instructions for Yuletide Fiesta begin on page 144.

Resplendent
in Red

Ring in the holidays with irresistible red! Flowing from the ceiling to the floor, shades of scarlet will make your home a warm, inviting space in which to entertain family and friends.

The amaryllis — long admired for bringing a dramatic show of color to winter — is a natural for holiday decorating. A hand-painted vase makes a beautiful container for an **Amaryllis Arrangement**.

Because nothing sets the mood like candlelight, hearts will be all aglow when they see this beautiful tablescape. Crisscross two Ribbon-Striped Table Runners (*opposite*) over a coffee table to lay the foundation for a festive centerpiece.

For a truly personal touch, trim your tree with ornaments you've made yourself (*above, left to right*). The Orange-Red Glass Ornaments are simply made by swirling a mixture of acrylic paint and matte medium inside clear glass ornaments. Looking like tiny wrapped gift boxes, the Fabric-Covered Canvas Ornaments are covered with assorted red fabrics and accented with ribbons or sequins and beads. Polka-Dotted Ornaments hung with ribbons will give your tree a playful touch.

Transform plain glass candleholders into works of art by hand painting them. Surround your Dotted and Striped Candleholders (*left*) with tea lights and silk amaryllis blossoms to complete this classy showpiece.

Instructions for Resplendent in Red begin on page 147.

Extra seating is always a must during the holiday season. These comfy Floor Cushions (*right*) are ideal for accommodating guests in style! For a striking combination of beauty and practicality, make some Fabric-Covered Boxes (*below*). They'll add a decorative touch, while concealing Christmas gifts. Simple to create, these Geometric Paintings (*opposite*) provide an instant burst of color to the wall and look great framing a traditional Red Wreath that's made from silk flowers. Infuse your home with inviting comfort by tossing a merry mixture of pillows onto the sofa. The Round Sequined Pillow, **Red Ribbon-Striped Pillow**, and Tufted Pillows offer delightful texture, while the luxurious Red Throw lends warmth.

Instructions for Resplendent in Red begin on page 147.

Grand Entrances

Guests and passersby will be mesmerized when they behold your **Blue & Bronze Entryway**. Adorned with fabric, ribbon, garland, and hand-crafted ornaments, Ribbon Trees lend drama to the entrance. A **Shimmering Swag** and two Beribboned Wreaths dress up the door.

Instructions for Grand Entrances begin on page 151.

Designed to resemble a scene from *A Christmas Carol*, this enchanting **Dickens Entry** will have everyone singing for joy. A grand **Swag Garland** trims the front door in timeless beauty, while large poinsettias add a natural burst of color. An **Evergreen Wreath** with music-note ribbon ties in beautifully with our caroling theme.

Instructions for Grand Entrances begin on page 151.

The **Wall Sconce Swag**, with its bounty of bright red berries, features the same music-stamped ribbon used on the wreath. A generous plaid bow tops off the splendid arrangement.

Instructions for Grand Entrances begin on page 151.

Instructions for Grand Entrances begin on page 151.

Life-size **Carolers** are in perfect harmony with this storybook setting. Our patterns will make creating the characters a cinch. Use old clothing and hats to bring the trio to life.

Light the way to Christmas cheer with **Lantern Luminaries** (*right*). Use greenery, berries, and ribbon to spruce up metal lanterns, then add coordinating candles for a warm holiday glow. A sleigh laden with **Outdoor Gift Boxes** (*below*) completes the festive ensemble.

Ribbon-Tied Luminaries (*above, left*) will make the season bright. Flank each side of the doorway with Wreath Topiaries (*left*) for a unique accent.

Instructions for Grand Entrances begin on page 151.

V isitors to your home will have their Christmas spirit sparked by
this Whimsical Entry. Draped around the doorway, Door Garland
with Jumbo Ornaments provides a festive frosting of holiday fun.
Accented with berry picks and glass ball ornaments, Column Greenery
grounds the ribbon-wrapped posts. Whimsical Door Wreaths
add the crowning touch to your entryway.

The Sharing

# of Christmas

Because it's made with love, a handcrafted gift is ideal for expressing seasonal sentiment. The following pages are filled with sleigh loads of thoughtful tokens to make for family, friends, co-workers, your child's teacher, and everyone else on your list. From fun-and-funky fashions and ribbon-wrapped decorations to flavorful appetizers and scrumptious sweets, this collection has you covered. We've even helped with the wrapping by including clever ideas for packaging your presents. So get ready to warm the hearts of all who are near and dear with the sharing of Christmas!

It is more blessed to give than to receive, so be especially blessed this Christmas by crafting these sure-to-please presents for friends and loved ones. Let them know they're the light of your life with pretty **Candle Jars**, or with any of the thoughtful gifts in this section.

Share the *spirit*

Instructions for Share the Spirit begin on page 156.

Wrap up holiday gift-giving with Beribboned Ornaments. A merry mixture of ribbons lends a decorative touch to otherwise simple baubles. The date tag is a thoughtful way to remind recipients of when you gave them the ornament.

Fashionable yet casual describes this beautiful **Button Bracelet** (*below*). By simply changing the color and style of the buttons, you can personalize the bracelet to suit anyone! Our **Beaded Brooch** is a gift that offers timeless appeal. The floral design is decidedly feminine.

Want to give a gift of glamour? These **Knit Collars** (*above and opposite*) are just the thing! Created using bulky weight novelty yarn and clasped with a brooch, the trendy accessories will add glitz to a young woman's wardrobe.

A Ribbon-Wrapped Wreath will dress a door in Victorian charm. The pretty accent is decorated with beaded garland and a vintage handkerchief, which is highlighted by flowing ribbon and an antique pin.

Instructions for Share the Spirit begin on page 156.

Surprise your favorite cook with a pair of festive **Appliquéd Tea Towels**. The handy holiday helpers will be appreciated during all the making and baking of the season. Buttons accent the cute appliquéd designs.

Let the jolly **Santa Box** deliver your season's greetings to a friend or co-worker. The hand-painted design highlights a wooden container that can be filled with your choice of goodies.

Fashion a **Framed Hankie** (*left*) for the antique admirer on your list. The vintage piece is dressed up with buttons, a collectible stamp, and a beribboned tag. Ideal for displaying cherished reminders of Christmases past, a **Framed Memorabilia** piece (*below*) is one of the most heartwarming gifts you can give a loved one.

Instructions for Share the Spirit *begin on page 156.*

WRAP UP
the holidays

You've chosen the perfect gift; now wrap it up in style by creating a clever container. From whimsical to elegant, these Christmas wrappings are as fun to make as they are to give.

This merry medley of wrappings will make your presents twice as nice. Recipients are sure to appreciate the containers as much as the gifts inside.

Recycle your collected Christmas cards by sewing them onto charming **Cotton Batting Bags** (*left*). The ancient art of paper folding takes on new form when used to make **Origami Boxes** (*opposite*). Decorate the folded boxes with scrapbook paper and assorted embellishments.

Capture the essence of winter with a frosty **Embossed Gift Bag and Tag**. Showy snowflakes drift across the pretty package and coordinating tag. For a textured touch, top the bag with a torn piece of blue vellum that has been embossed with a seasonal sentiment.

Kids of all ages will love these playful **Pinch Boxes** (*right*). Be sure to add the "Do Not Open Until Christmas" tags to ward off pre-Christmas peeking. An artful Yuletide tree appliqué accents a fetching **Felt Bag** (*below, left*).

Our simple patterns will make easy work of transforming plain Bristol board into a beautiful **Folded Box**. Enhance the container with gilded flourishes.

Fashioned from manila tags, this **Two-Tag Gift Holder** (*right*) is cute and clever. A **Decorated Envelope** (*below*) is the ideal package for a thin gift — such as a calendar, a sentimental photograph, or a "homemade" coupon book.

Merry Christmas

To Barbara
From Polly

Christmas Wish

merry Munchies to share

For gifts they're sure to enjoy, deliver delectable delights to friends and family this Christmas. With palate-pleasing recipes for every taste, you're sure to find the ideal offering. Double their pleasure by presenting the merry munchies in handcrafted containers.

Instructions for Merry Munchies to Share begin on page 163.

TO
Kim
FROM
Lori

HAPPY
HOLIDAYS!

SPICED
CIDER

Merry Christmas

Cheese
Cookie
Snacks

SPICED CIDER MIX

Include a bag of cinnamon candies to complete this special treat.

- 1 cup orange breakfast drink mix
- 1 cup sugar
- $^1/_2$ cup instant tea
- 1 package (4 ounces) sweetened lemonade drink mix
- $^1/_2$ teaspoon ground cinnamon
- $^1/_4$ teaspoon ground cloves
- $^1/_4$ teaspoon ground allspice

Combine orange breakfast drink mix and remaining ingredients together in a large bowl, stirring well. Store in an airtight container. Mix can be frozen up to 1 month.
Yield: Makes 3 cups mix

Serving Instructions: Combine 3 tablespoons Spiced Cider Mix, 1 teaspoon cinnamon candies, and 1 cup boiling water. Stir well.

A unique blend of flavors — orange and lemon drink mixes, instant tea, and spices — gives Spiced Cider Mix *(above, right)* its zing! Tuck the mix into a festively decorated Wrapped Mug for a quick-to-fix gift. Deliver holiday wishes with a **Cookie Card** *(above)* that you've topped with a scrumptious Peppermint Cookie.

PEPPERMINT COOKIES

- $^1/_2$ cup butter, softened
- $^1/_2$ cup butter-flavored shortening or regular shortening
- $1^1/_2$ cups sugar
- 1 large egg
- $1^1/_2$ teaspoons peppermint extract
- $^1/_2$ teaspoon vanilla extract
- $3^1/_2$ cups sifted cake flour
- $1^1/_2$ teaspoons baking powder
- $^1/_4$ teaspoon salt
- $^3/_4$ teaspoon red paste food coloring

Beat butter and shortening at medium speed with an electric mixer until creamy; gradually add sugar, beating well. Add egg, beating well. Stir in flavorings. Combine flour, baking powder, and salt; add to butter mixture, beating well. Remove half of dough from bowl. Add food coloring to dough in bowl, and mix until color is evenly distributed.

Working with half of each dough at a time, shape plain dough by teaspoonfuls into 4-inch ropes. (Cover remaining dough to prevent drying.) Repeat shaping with red dough. Place 1 red rope and 1 plain rope side by side; carefully twist together. Roll twisted ropes into 1 smooth rope; shape rope into a tightly coiled cookie. Repeat with remaining dough. Chill 15 minutes.

Place cookies on ungreased cookie sheets. Bake at 375° for 8 minutes or just until cookies begin to brown. Cool slightly; carefully remove cookies to wire racks, using a wide spatula, and cool completely.
Yield: about 4 dozen cookies

W hat better way to offer "Nutcracker Sweets" than in a canister that resembles a toy soldier nutcracker? Using our patterns, you can easily transform a plain snack chip container into an enchanting gift.

Instructions for Merry Munchies to Share begin on page 163.

NUTCRACKER SWEETS
These will remind you of traditional wedding cookies or sand tarts with cherries.

    1   cup butter, softened
  ¹/₄   cup granulated sugar
    2   cups all-purpose flour
    2   cups ground almonds
  ¹/₄   teaspoon almond extract
  ¹/₄   cup maraschino cherries, drained and chopped
        Powdered sugar

Beat butter and sugar at medium speed with an electric mixer until creamy. Add flour, almonds, and extract, beating at low speed until well blended. Stir in cherries.

Shape dough into 1-inch balls. Place on ungreased baking sheets.

Bake at 325° for 18 to 22 minutes or until lightly browned. Remove to wire racks; cool 2 minutes. Roll cookies in powdered sugar; cool completely on wire racks.
Yield: Makes 3¹/₂ to 4 dozen cookies

"Espress" your feelings by making **Espresso Fudge** for family and friends. Place the temptingly rich tidbits in a dressed-up shirt box that you've embellished with curly paper-strip ribbons and a papier-mâché star.

ESPRESSO FUDGE

Espresso granules have abundant flavor that mellows with hazelnuts and chocolate cookie crumbs. This recipe is so rich you'll want to cut it into tiny squares.

- 10   chocolate cookies with cream filling
- ¹/₄   cup instant espresso granules, divided
- 1¹/₂   cups sugar
- ¹/₂   cup butter or margarine
- 1   can (5 ounces) evaporated milk
- 8   ounces vanilla-flavored candy coating, chopped
- 1   jar (7 ounces) marshmallow cream
- ¹/₂   cup chopped hazelnuts
- 1   teaspoon vanilla extract

Position cutting blade in food processor bowl. Add cookies and 2 tablespoons espresso granules; process until mixture resembles fine crumbs. Set aside.

Line a 13 x 9 x 2-inch pan with a large sheet of aluminum foil, allowing foil to extend 1 inch beyond ends of pan. Butter the foil and set aside.

Combine remaining 2 tablespoons espresso granules, sugar, ¹/₂ cup butter, and milk in a large saucepan. Cook over low heat until sugar and espresso granules dissolve, stirring occasionally. Bring to a boil over medium heat, stirring constantly. Boil 5 minutes, stirring constantly, until mixture reaches soft ball stage or candy thermometer registers 234°. Remove from heat.

Add candy coating and marshmallow cream, stirring until candy coating melts. Stir in hazelnuts and vanilla. Gently fold in reserved cookie crumb mixture, creating a speckled effect.

Spread mixture into prepared pan. Let cool completely. Carefully lift foil out of pan. Cut fudge into small squares.
Yield: 2 pounds fudge

CHUNKS OF SNOW

- 1   pound white chocolate candy coating, chopped
- 1   jar (3.5 ounces) macadamia nuts
- 1   package (6 ounces) sweetened dried cranberries

Melt candy coating in a saucepan over low heat, stirring constantly. Remove from heat; stir in nuts and dried cranberries. Spread mixture onto a lightly greased baking sheet. Cool. Break into pieces.
Yield: 1¹/₂ pounds candy

CARAMEL SAUCE

- 1/2 cup butter or margarine
- 1 1/4 cups firmly packed brown sugar
- 2 tablespoons light corn syrup
- 1/2 cup whipping cream

Melt butter in a small heavy saucepan over low heat; add sugar and corn syrup. Bring to a boil; cook, stirring constantly, 1 minute or until sugar dissolves. Gradually add cream; return to a boil. Cool completely. Give with Gingerbread Spoons.

Yield: 2 cups sauce

GINGERBREAD SPOONS

These edible spoons are delicious served with ice cream and Caramel Sauce.

- 1/2 cup butter or margarine, softened
- 3/4 cup firmly packed dark brown sugar
- 1 large egg
- 1/3 cup molasses
- 2 1/2 tablespoons lemon juice
- 3 to 3 1/2 cups all-purpose flour, divided
- 1 tablespoon baking powder
- 1/4 teaspoon baking soda
   Dash of salt
- 1 1/2 teaspoons ground ginger
- 1 teaspoon ground cinnamon
- 1/4 teaspoon ground cloves

Beat butter at medium speed with an electric mixer until creamy; gradually add brown sugar, beating well. Add egg, molasses, and lemon juice; beat well.

Combine 1 cup flour and next 6 ingredients; stir well. Add to butter mixture, beating until blended. Gradually add enough remaining flour to make a stiff dough. Cover and chill dough 1 hour.

Divide dough into 2 portions. Roll each portion on a lightly greased cookie sheet to 1/4-inch thickness; cover and freeze until firm.

Using a standard tablespoon as a pattern, trace spoons onto dough with a sharp knife, about 2 inches apart. Remove excess dough from cookie sheet.

Repeat procedure with remaining frozen dough. Combine scraps of dough and repeat procedure until all dough is used.

Bake at 350° for 10 minutes or until golden. Let cool 1 minute on cookie sheets. Remove to wire racks; let cookies cool completely.

Yield: about 3 1/2 dozen spoons

For a gift that's twice as nice, tie Gingerbread Spoons (*above*) onto a jar filled with creamy Caramel Sauce. Chunks of Snow (*below*) are a tasty tribute to winter! Share the wonder by decorating a reusable container with snowflakes and a frosty friend.

Instructions for Merry Munchies to Share begin on page 163.

SPICED PEAR JAM

    8 cups peeled, finely chopped ripe pears (about
         5 1/2 pounds)
    4 cups sugar
    1 teaspoon ground cinnamon
  1/4 teaspoon ground cloves

Bring all ingredients to a boil in a Dutch oven, stirring constantly. Reduce heat; simmer, stirring occasionally, 2 hours or until thickened. Skim off foam with a metal spoon.

Pour immediately into hot jars, leaving 1/4-inch headspace; wipe jar rims. Cover at once with metal lids, and screw on bands.

Process in a boiling-water bath 10 minutes.
Yield: 5 half-pints jam

RED ZINGER JELLY

1 3/4 cups water
   12 regular-size Red Zinger® tea bags
  1/4 cup fresh orange juice
    3 cups sugar
    2 tablespoons grated orange rind
    2 teaspoons orange liqueur (optional)
    1 package (3 ounces) liquid pectin

Bring 1 3/4 cups water to a boil in a large saucepan; pour over tea bags. Cover and steep 20 minutes. Discard tea bags.

Pour orange juice through a fine wire-mesh strainer into saucepan, discarding pulp. Stir in brewed tea, sugar, orange rind, and, if desired, liqueur; bring to a boil. Boil, stirring constantly, 2 minutes. Remove from heat, and cool 5 minutes.

Stir liquid pectin into tea mixture; cooking over medium-low heat, return to a boil, and boil, stirring constantly, 1 minute. Remove from heat, and skim off foam with a metal spoon.

Pour hot jelly into hot sterilized jars, filling to 1/4 inch from top; wipe jar rims. Cover at once with metal lids, and screw on bands.

Process in boiling-water bath 5 minutes, or store in refrigerator up to 3 months.
Yield: 3 half-pints jelly

P reserve holiday cheer with a gift that keeps giving beyond Christmas … a jar of Spiced Pear Jam (*opposite*) or Red Zinger Jelly presented in a "quilted" gift bag. Whimsically labeled **Citrus Party Olives** (*right*) are treasures for the taste buds. They also make an ideal hostess gift.

CITRUS PARTY OLIVES

    4 garlic cloves, chopped
  1/2 cup olive oil
    1 tablespoon grated orange rind
    2 teaspoons grated lemon rind
  1/3 cup fresh orange juice
    3 tablespoons fresh lemon juice
1 1/2 teaspoons chopped fresh rosemary
    1 teaspoon coarse salt
  1/2 teaspoon freshly ground pepper
    4 cans (6 ounces each) ripe pitted black olives,
         drained

Stir together all ingredients in a large bowl. Cover and chill at least 8 hours.

Spoon olives into large jars to give as gifts. Keep refrigerated.
Yield: 6 servings

Serving Instructions: Store in refrigerator. Let stand 30 minutes at room temperature before serving. Garnish, if desired, with fresh rosemary sprigs. Serve with a slotted spoon or on toothpicks.

Instructions for Merry Munchies to Share begin on page 163.

Cheese Cookie Snacks (*above*) are an excellent alternative to sugary sweet cookies, making it a thoughtful token for someone who has to watch what they eat. A cleverly crafted Snack Tube makes a cute package for the cookies. Share a sentimental moment with someone special this Christmas by hand-stitching a Kitchen Towel Bag (*opposite*) and embellishing it with a favorite photo. For an appetizing offering, put in a loaf of fresh bread and a jar of Pecan Pimiento Cheese.

CHEESE COOKIE SNACKS

- 1 cup (4 ounces) shredded Cheddar cheese
- $1/2$ cup butter or margarine, softened
- 1 cup all-purpose flour
- $1/4$ teaspoon salt
- 1 cup crisp rice cereal

Stir together cheese and butter until blended. Stir in flour and salt; blend well. Stir in cereal. (Dough will be stiff.)

Shape dough into 1-inch balls; place on an ungreased baking sheet 2 inches apart. Flatten cookies to $1/4$-inch thickness with a fork, making a crisscross.

Bake at 350° for 15 to 18 minutes. Remove to wire rack to cool. Store in an airtight container.
Yield: about 2 dozen cookies

PECAN PIMIENTO CHEESE

- $1 1/2$ cups mayonnaise
- 1 jar (4 ounces) diced pimiento, drained
- 1 teaspoon Worchestershire sauce
- 1 tablespoon finely grated onion
- $1/4$ teaspoon ground red pepper
- 8 ounces extra-sharp Cheddar cheese, finely shredded
- 8 ounces sharp Cheddar cheese, shredded
- $3/4$ cup chopped pecans, toasted

Stir together first five ingredients in a bowl; stir in cheeses and pecans. Store in refrigerator up to 1 week.
Yield: 4 cups cheese

Instructions for Merry Munchies to Share begin on page 163.

We aUnt Jane's

Pecan Pimiento Cheese

The Tastes

# of Christmas

Good food and good cheer mean the holidays are here! A season of celebration, Christmas presents us with a myriad of opportunities to fellowship with friends and family over delicious meals. Our selection of menus and recipes was chosen with the many different needs of today's families in mind. On a special diet? Try our low-carb selections. Too busy to cook? Plan a round-robin with your neighbors. Or perhaps you want to make a difference in someone's life? Host a knitting bee luncheon to help your friends make an afghan for charity. Whatever the season holds, savor the tastes of Christmas!

Knitting Bee Luncheon

Invite your friends over for a fun and meaningful get-together to create an afghan that will warm someone in need — in body and in spirit! Include in your invitation the instructions for knitting squares, and have each guest bring several completed squares to the party. After lunch, everyone will sew the squares together into a patchwork blanket. The completed afghan can be donated locally or sent to the Warm Up America! Foundation, which distributes afghans to battered women's shelters, nursing homes, homeless shelters, and other relief organizations.

Instructions for Invitation and Knitted Squares are on page 167.

ALL-SEASON FRUIT SALAD

    1   pint fresh strawberries, sliced
1 1/2   cups seedless green grapes
    1   cup honeydew melon balls
    2   oranges, peeled, seeded, and sectioned
    2   kiwifruit, peeled and sliced
    1   apple, unpeeled, cored, and sliced
  1/4   cup orange juice
    2   tablespoons honey
    1   tablespoon lime juice
    2   bananas, sliced

Combine first 6 ingredients in a large bowl.

Combine orange juice, honey, and lime juice; pour over fruit in bowl, tossing gently. Cover and chill 2 hours. Add banana just before serving.

Yield: 12 servings

GINGERED CITRUS COOLER

    1   quart apple juice, divided
    1   lime, thinly sliced
    1   jar (2.7 ounces) crystallized ginger
    1   quart pineapple juice
    1   quart orange juice

Combine 2 cups apple juice, lime, and ginger in a small saucepan. Bring to a boil; reduce heat and simmer, uncovered, 3 minutes. Remove from heat; cover and let cool.

Strain juice mixture into a pitcher; discard ginger and lime. Stir in remaining 2 cups apple juice, pineapple juice, and orange juice; chill thoroughly.

Yield: 3 quarts cooler

Note: For a Rum-Spiked Cooler, mix 4 parts Gingered Citrus Cooler with 1 part golden rum.

The best part of working on a Warm Up America! afghan is seeing what friends can accomplish when they work together. To make sure your group of volunteers has plenty of energy for the task, start lunch with an All-Season Fruit Salad and a **Gingered Citrus Cooler.**

CUCUMBER-DILL SOUP

2 cucumbers, peeled, seeded, and coarsely chopped
1 green onion, coarsely chopped
1 tablespoon lemon juice
1 container (16 ounces) sour cream (see Note)
1 cup half-and-half (see Note)
1 tablespoon minced fresh dill
1 teaspoon salt
$^1/_4$ teaspoon pepper
$^1/_8$ teaspoon hot sauce
   Garnish: fresh dill sprigs or chives

Process first 3 ingredients in a blender or food processor until smooth, stopping to scrape down sides. Pour into a large bowl; stir in sour cream and next 5 ingredients. Cover and chill 2 hours. Garnish soup, if desired.
Yield: 4 cups soup
Note: One container (16 ounces) light sour cream and 1 cup fat-free half-and-half may be substituted.

Guests will enjoy the refreshingly rich flavor of cool **Cucumber-Dill Soup**. For the main event, serve Chicken-Wild Rice Salad. The light, yet filling salad is just right for lunch.

CHICKEN-WILD RICE SALAD

1 cup mayonnaise
2 tablespoons minced fresh dill
2 tablespoons lemon juice
2 teaspoons curry powder
6 cups chopped cooked chicken
4 cups cooked wild rice, chilled
1 cup frozen English peas, thawed
1 cup chopped carrot
1 cup minced green onions
4 tablespoons diced pimiento, drained
1 teaspoon salt
$^1/_2$ teaspoon pepper
$^1/_4$ teaspoon garlic powder
   Green leaf lettuce leaves
   Garnish: cherry tomatoes

Combine first 4 ingredients in a large bowl; stir well. Add chicken and next 8 ingredients; stir well. Cover and chill at least 1 hour. Spoon evenly onto individual lettuce-lined salad plates, and garnish, if desired.
Yield: 12 servings

HAM AND CRANBERRY CREAM CHEESE SANDWICHES

Four ingredients become delicious holiday finger sandwiches with only a few minutes work.

$^1/_2$ cup tub-style cream cheese, softened
$^1/_2$ cup whole-berry cranberry sauce
28 slices cinnamon-raisin bread, crusts removed
28 very thin slices smoked ham (1$^1/_4$ pounds)

Combine cream cheese and cranberry sauce, stirring well. Spread a heaping teaspoon cream cheese mixture onto each bread slice. Top half of bread slices with 2 slices ham. Place remaining bread, cream cheese side down, onto ham. Cut each sandwich into 4 triangles using a sharp knife.
Yield: 14 servings

PARMESAN CHEESE ROUNDS

- ²/₃ cup packaged shredded Parmesan cheese (see Note)
- ½ cup butter or margarine, softened
- 1 cup all-purpose flour
- ¼ teaspoon salt
- ¼ teaspoon ground red pepper
  Pecan halves (optional)

Position cutting blade in food processor bowl; add cheese and butter. Process until blended. Add flour, salt, and ground red pepper; process about 30 seconds or until mixture forms a ball, stopping often to scrape down sides.

Shape dough into ¾-inch balls; flatten each ball to about ⅛-inch thickness. Place on ungreased baking sheets; top with pecan halves, if desired.

Bake at 350° for 10 minutes or until lightly browned. Transfer to wire racks to cool.

Yield: 3 dozen rounds

Note: You can substitute ²/₃ cup freshly grated Parmesan cheese plus an additional ¼ cup all-purpose flour for the packaged shredded Parmesan cheese.

As appealing to the eyes as they are to the taste buds, Ham and Cranberry Cream Cheese Sandwiches are easier to make than they appear! Pecan-topped Parmesan Cheese Rounds are ideal for nibbling.

merry MORNING *brunch*

After a merry morning spent opening Christmas presents, treat your family to a host of soon-to-be brunch favorites. Everyone will be pleased with this flavorful assortment of breakfast breads and spreads.

Taste buds will wake up and take notice of this Cranberry Crunch Coffee Cake. Packed with cranberries and walnuts, the coffee cake is a natural choice for Christmas brunch.

CRANBERRY CRUNCH COFFEE CAKE

⅔ cup butter or margarine, softened
1 cup granulated sugar
1 cup firmly packed light brown sugar, divided
½ cup egg substitute
2 cups all-purpose flour
1½ teaspoons ground cinnamon, divided
1 teaspoon baking powder
1 teaspoon baking soda
½ teaspoon salt
1 cup buttermilk
½ teaspoon ground nutmeg
¾ cup coarsely chopped walnuts
1¾ cups fresh or frozen cranberries, minced

Beat butter at medium speed with an electric mixer until creamy; gradually add granulated sugar and ½ cup brown sugar, beating well. Add egg substitute, beating well.

Combine flour, 1 teaspoon cinnamon, and next 3 ingredients; add to butter mixture alternately with buttermilk, beginning and ending with flour mixture. Mix well after each addition. Spoon half of batter into a greased and floured 13 x 9-inch pan.

Combine remaining ½ cup brown sugar, remaining ½ teaspoon cinnamon, nutmeg, and walnuts; sprinkle half of mixture over batter, and top with cranberries. Dollop with remaining batter, and sprinkle with remaining brown sugar mixture.

Bake at 350° for 35 to 40 minutes or until a wooden pick inserted in center comes out clean. Cut into squares, and serve coffee cake warm.
Yield: 12 to 15 servings

HAM AND CHEESE MUFFINS

2½ cups biscuit and baking mix
¾ cup diced cooked ham (for maximum flavor, use country ham)
¾ cup shredded sharp Cheddar cheese
¾ cup half-and-half
3 tablespoons vegetable oil
1 large egg, lightly beaten

Combine baking mix, ham, and cheese in a large bowl. Make a well in center of mixture. Combine half-and-half, oil, and egg; add to dry ingredients, stirring just until dry ingredients are moistened.

Spoon into greased muffin pans, filling three-fourths full. Bake at 400° for 11 to 12 minutes or until a wooden pick inserted into center comes out clean. Remove from pans immediately.
Yield: 1 dozen muffins

GRAHAM CRACKER BREAD

1 package dry yeast
¼ cup warm water (100° to 110°)
2 cups all-purpose flour
¾ cup cinnamon graham cracker crumbs (about 5 full cracker sheets)
½ cup whole-wheat flour
2 tablespoons honey
½ teaspoon grated orange rind
½ teaspoon salt
2 tablespoons chilled stick margarine, cut into small pieces
⅔ cup warm water (100° to 110°; see Note)
2 tablespoons all-purpose flour
Cooking spray

Dissolve yeast in ¼ cup warm water; let stand 5 minutes.

Place 2 cups all-purpose flour and next 5 ingredients (all-purpose flour through salt) in a food processor; pulse 4 times. Add margarine; process 10 seconds. With processor on, slowly add yeast mixture and ⅔ cup water through food chute; process until combined. With processor on, add 2 tablespoons all-purpose flour through food chute, 1 tablespoon at a time, until dough leaves sides of bowl and forms a ball. Process 15 additional seconds.

Place dough in a large bowl coated with cooking spray, turning to coat top. Cover and let rise in a warm place (85°), free from drafts, 45 minutes or until doubled in bulk. Punch dough down; divide into 3 equal portions. Working with one portion at a time (cover remaining dough to keep from drying), shape each portion into a 12-inch rope. Place 3 ropes lengthwise on a large baking sheet; pinch ends together at one end to seal. Braid ropes; pinch loose ends to seal. Place in an 8 x 4-inch loaf pan coated with cooking spray. Cover and let rise 45 minutes or until doubled in bulk.

Preheat oven to 375°. Bake at 375° for 30 minutes or until loaf sounds hollow when tapped. Remove from pan immediately; cool on a wire rack.
Yield: 1 loaf bread
Note: When using a bread machine, increase second listing of water from ⅔ cup to 1 cup; follow manufacturer's instructions for placing all dough ingredients in bread pan. Select cycle, and start bread machine.

Easy-to-make, these **Ham and Cheese Muffins** will satisfy hearty appetites. Baking mix helps you prepare the breakfast delights in a flash.

CHIVE 'N' CHEDDAR DROP BISCUITS

- 3 cups biscuit and baking mix
- 1 cup (4 ounces) finely shredded sharp Cheddar cheese
- 1 tablespoon chopped fresh or dried chives
- 1/2 teaspoon garlic powder
- 1 cup milk
- 1/2 cup sour cream
- 3 tablespoons butter, melted

Combine first 4 ingredients in a large bowl; make a well in center of mixture.

Combine milk and sour cream; add to dry ingredients, stirring just until dry ingredients are moistened.

Drop by 1/4 cupfuls onto a lightly greased baking sheet; brush with butter. Bake at 425° for 8 to 10 minutes or until golden. Brush with any remaining butter before serving.
Yield: 15 biscuits

BUTTERMILK-OATMEAL BREAD

- 2 envelopes (1/4 ounce each) active dry yeast
- 1/4 cup warm water (100° to 110°)
- 1 3/4 cups water
- 1/2 cup butter or margarine
- 1 cup uncooked quick-cooking oats
- 1 1/2 teaspoons salt
- 2 tablespoons molasses
- 1 cup buttermilk
- 3 cups whole wheat flour
- 2 1/2 to 3 cups bread flour

Combine yeast and 1/4 cup warm water in a 1-cup liquid measuring cup; let stand 5 minutes.

Cook 1 3/4 cups water and next 3 ingredients in a large saucepan over medium heat until butter melts. Stir in molasses and buttermilk; cool to 100° to 110°. Stir in yeast mixture.

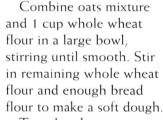

Combine oats mixture and 1 cup whole wheat flour in a large bowl, stirring until smooth. Stir in remaining whole wheat flour and enough bread flour to make a soft dough.

Turn dough out onto a well-floured surface, and knead until smooth and elastic (10 to 15 minutes). Place in a well-greased bowl, turning to grease top.

Cover and let rise in a warm place (85°), free from drafts, 1 hour or until doubled in bulk.

Punch dough down, and divide in half; shape each portion into a loaf. Place into 2 greased 8 1/2 x 4 1/2-inch loaf pans.

Cover and let rise in a warm place, free from drafts, 30 minutes or until doubled in bulk.

Bake at 350° for 30 minutes or until golden brown. Remove from pans immediately, and cool on wire racks.
Yield: 2 loaves bread

BLUEBERRY BISCUITS

 ½ cup frozen blueberries, thawed
 2 cups all-purpose flour
 2 teaspoons baking powder
 ¼ teaspoon baking soda
 1 teaspoon salt
 ½ cup sugar
 ⅓ cup shortening
 1 large egg
 ¾ cup buttermilk
 3 tablespoons butter or margarine, melted
 2 tablespoons sugar
 ¼ teaspoon ground cinnamon

Pat blueberries dry with paper towels; set aside.

Combine flour and next 4 ingredients in a large bowl; cut in shortening with a pastry blender until crumbly.

Whisk together egg and buttermilk; add to flour mixture, stirring just until dry ingredients are moistened. Gently fold in blueberries.

Turn dough out onto a lightly floured surface; knead 3 or 4 times.

Pat or roll dough to ¾-inch thickness; cut with a 2¾-inch round cutter, and place on a lightly greased baking sheet.

Bake at 400° for 15 minutes or until biscuits are golden brown. Stir together butter, 2 tablespoons sugar and cinnamon; brush mixture over warm biscuits.

Yield: 8 biscuits

Note: Recipe can be doubled. Freeze biscuits in an airtight container for up to 3 weeks.

These Blueberry Biscuits can be frozen for up to three weeks, so make them ahead of time and you won't have to miss out on Christmas morning festivities.

BACON MONKEY BREAD

 11 bacon slices, cooked and crumbled
 ½ cup grated Parmesan cheese
 1 small onion, chopped
 3 cans (10 ounces each) refrigerated buttermilk
    biscuits
 ½ cup butter or margarine, melted

Combine first 3 ingredients, and set aside.

Cut each biscuit into fourths. Dip one-third of biscuit pieces into melted butter, and place in a lightly greased 10-inch Bundt® pan. Sprinkle with half of bacon mixture. Repeat layers with remaining biscuit pieces and bacon mixture, ending with biscuit pieces.

Bake at 350° for 40 minutes or until golden. Cool in pan 10 minutes; invert onto a serving platter, and serve bread immediately.

Yield: one 10-inch bread ring

BLACKBERRY BUTTER

 2 to 3 tablespoons seedless blackberry jam
 ½ cup softened butter

Stir the blackberry jam into the butter.

Yield: about ½ cup blackberry butter

WAFFLES

- 2 cups biscuit and baking mix
- 1/2 cup vegetable oil
- 2 large eggs
- 1 cup club soda

Stir together first 3 ingredients in a large bowl; add club soda, stirring until batter is blended.

Cook in a preheated, oiled waffle iron until golden.

Yield: ten 4-inch waffles

APRICOT BUTTER

- 1/2 cup butter or margarine, softened
- 1/4 cup honey
- 1/4 cup finely chopped dried apricots
- 1/2 teaspoon grated lemon rind

Beat butter at medium speed with an electric mixer until fluffy; add remaining ingredients, beating until blended. Chill, if desired.

Yield: 3/4 cup apricot butter

Get the family in on the fun of making Waffles *(right)*, then top the waffles with a fruit butter or syrup. A palate-pleasing spread, **Spiced Oven Apple Butter** *(below)* tastes great on toast, biscuits, and muffins.

SPICED OVEN APPLE BUTTER

- 8 Granny Smith apples, peeled and diced
- 1 cup apple juice
- 1 cup sugar
- 2 teaspoons cinnamon
- 1/2 teaspoon ground cloves
- 1/4 teaspoon ground allspice

Cook diced apples and juice in a Dutch oven over medium heat 20 to 30 minutes or until apples are tender. Stir until apples are mashed. Stir in the remaining ingredients. Pour apple mixture into a lightly greased 11 x 7-inch baking dish.

Bake at 275° for 4 1/2 hours, stirring every hour, or until spreading consistency. Let cool; cover and chill.

Yield: 3 cups apple butter

Coffeehouse
Christmas

Don't let a fun-filled day of holiday shopping with friends end at the mall. Invite them over for an evening of gift wrapping and unwinding! Our offering of coffeehouse-inspired beverages and decadent desserts will create the perfect ending to your day.

For a little taste of heaven, whip up a batch of these **Heavenly Chocolate Chunk Cookies**. Guests will be in for a sumptuous surprise when they taste your **Chocolate Chip-Cinnamon Biscotti**.

CHOCOLATE CHIP-CINNAMON BISCOTTI

- 1/3 cup butter or margarine, softened
- 1/2 cup firmly packed brown sugar
- 1/2 cup granulated sugar
- 1 tablespoon instant coffee or espresso granules
- 2 large eggs
- 2 cups all-purpose flour
- 1 1/2 teaspoons baking powder
- 1/8 teaspoon salt
- 1/2 teaspoon ground cinnamon
- 1 cup chopped walnuts or pecans
- 1 cup semisweet chocolate mini-morsels
- 4 ounces vanilla-flavored candy coating, melted

Combine first 4 ingredients in a large bowl; beat at medium speed with an electric mixer until light and fluffy. Add eggs, 1 at a time, beating until blended.

Combine flour and next 3 ingredients; add to butter mixture, stirring until blended. Fold in nuts and chocolate morsels. Divide dough in half, and shape each dough portion into a 10 x 2-inch log on a lightly greased baking sheet. Bake at 350° for 25 minutes or until firm.

Cool on baking sheet 5 minutes. Remove to wire racks to cool completely. Cut each log diagonally into 1/2-inch-thick slices with a serrated knife using a gentle sawing motion, and place slices, cut side up, on ungreased baking sheets. Bake slices at 350° for 10 minutes; turn cookies over, and bake 10 additional minutes. Remove cookies to wire racks to cool completely.

Dip 1 end of each cookie into candy coating; chill until set.
Yield: 2 1/2 dozen biscotti

HEAVENLY CHOCOLATE CHUNK COOKIES

Mega-morsels give a big chocolate taste to every bite of these deluxe chocolate chip cookies.

- 2 cups plus 2 tablespoons all-purpose flour
- 1/2 teaspoon baking soda
- 1/2 teaspoon salt
- 3/4 cup butter or margarine
- 2 tablespoons instant coffee granules
- 1 cup firmly packed brown sugar
- 1/2 cup granulated sugar
- 1 large egg
- 1 egg yolk
- 1 package (11.5 ounces) semisweet chocolate mega-morsels or chunks
- 1 cup walnut halves, toasted

Combine first 3 ingredients; stir well.

Combine butter and coffee granules in a small saucepan or skillet. Cook over medium-low heat until butter melts and coffee granules dissolve, stirring occasionally. Remove from heat, and let cool to room temperature (don't let butter resolidify).

Combine butter mixture, sugars, egg, and egg yolk in a large bowl. Beat at medium speed with an electric mixer until blended. Gradually add flour mixture, beating at low speed just until blended. Stir in mega-morsels and walnuts.

Drop dough by heaping tablespoonfuls 2 inches apart onto ungreased cookie sheets. Bake at 325° for 12 to 14 minutes. Let cool slightly on cookie sheets. Remove to wire racks to cool completely.
Yield: about 27 cookies

SLICE 'N' BAKE COFFEE COOKIES

- 1/2 cup unsalted butter, softened
- 1 cup sugar
- 1 large egg
- 1 teaspoon vanilla extract
- 2 cups all-purpose flour
- 1 teaspoon baking powder
- 1/4 teaspoon salt
- 3/4 cup toasted and skinned whole hazelnuts, chopped
- 1/4 cup sugar
- 1 tablespoon hazelnut-flavored instant coffee granules

Beat butter at medium speed with an electric mixer until creamy; gradually add 1 cup sugar, beating well. Add egg and vanilla, beating until blended.

Combine flour, baking powder, and salt; add to butter mixture, beating well. Stir in hazelnuts. Divide dough in half; shape into 11-inch logs.

Combine 1/4 cup sugar and coffee granules; stir well. Roll each log in sugar mixture, coating heavily. Wrap each log in wax paper. Chill logs until firm.

Cut dough into 1/4-inch-thick slices, and place on ungreased cookie sheets. Bake at 350° for 8 to 10 minutes or until lightly browned. Remove to wire racks, and cool completely. Store in an airtight container up to 1 week.
Yield: 6 dozen cookies

Rich and refreshing, a cold mug of **Frosted Coffee** is a delicious alternative to the usual hot beverage.

FROSTED COFFEE

You can double this thick, icy concoction to serve a crowd; just be sure to prepare it in batches. Spoon immediately into frosty pitchers for serving — it melts quickly.

    3   cups coffee ice cream
    1/4 cup hot fudge topping
    1/4 teaspoon ground cinnamon
    3   cups small ice cubes
        Garnish: maraschino cherries with stems

Combine first 3 ingredients in container of an electric blender; cover and process just until blended, stopping once to scrape down sides. Turn blender on high; gradually add ice, blending until smooth. Garnish, if desired. Serve immediately.
Yield: 4 cups frosted coffee

MOCHA POUND CAKE

    2   teaspoons instant coffee granules
    2   teaspoons hot water
    1/2 cup butter, softened
    2   cups sifted powdered sugar
    1   pound cake (10 ounces)
    1   jar (3.5 ounces) macadamia nuts,
          chopped (see Note)
    1   quart vanilla ice cream
    3/4 to 1 cup chocolate sauce
    3/4 to 1 cup caramel sauce

Dissolve coffee granules in hot water.
Beat butter at medium speed with an electric mixer until creamy; gradually add sugar, beating until light and fluffy. Add coffee, and beat until spreading consistency. Set frosting aside.
Trim crust from cake. Cut cake into 6 pieces. Spread frosting on top and sides of pieces; roll in nuts. Top with ice cream, and drizzle with sauces.
Yield: 6 servings
Note: You can substitute 3/4 cup chopped cocktail peanuts for the macadamia nuts.

Frosted and rolled in nuts, an ordinary pound cake becomes irresistible Mocha Pound Cake. The nutty-sweet creation is topped off with ice cream and drizzled with caramel and chocolate sauce.

RUM-GLAZED COFFEE ROLLS

Don't worry about how you arrange these sugar-coated biscuits in the pan — during baking they expand into a coffee cake that separates easily into single rolls.

- ½ cup coarsely chopped pecans
- 1 cup firmly packed brown sugar
- ⅓ cup brewed coffee
- ¼ cup butter or margarine, melted
- 2 tablespoons dark rum
- ⅔ cup granulated sugar
- 2 tablespoons instant coffee granules
- 2 cans (11 ounces each) refrigerated buttermilk biscuits
- ⅓ cup butter or margarine, melted

Sprinkle pecans in a heavily greased 12-cup Bundt® pan. Combine brown sugar and next 3 ingredients, stirring well. Pour mixture into pan.

Combine granulated sugar and coffee granules in a shallow bowl; stir well. Separate biscuits; dip biscuits in melted butter, and dredge in sugar mixture. Stand biscuits on edge around pan, placing 12 on outer side and 8 on inner side of pan.

Bake at 350° for 28 to 33 minutes. Cool in pan on a wire rack 5 minutes. Invert onto a serving platter, and serve immediately.
Yield: 20 rolls

HOT COCOA

- ⅓ cup sugar
- ¼ cup cocoa
  Pinch of salt
- ½ cup water
- 4 cups milk
- ¼ teaspoon vanilla extract
  Sweetened whipped cream
  Grated sweet baking chocolate

Combine first 3 ingredients in a heavy saucepan. Add water, and bring to a boil over medium heat, stirring constantly. Stir in milk, and heat thoroughly (do not boil). Stir in vanilla. Serve cocoa topped with whipped cream and grated chocolate.
Yield: 4½ cups cocoa

Set out **Rum-Glazed Coffee Rolls** and watch them disappear! An ideal complement to the pull-apart sweet bread, a cup of homemade Hot Cocoa will warm both body and soul.

Make your at-home coffeehouse get-together complete by serving a selection of flavorful beverages, such as these Cappuccino Sippers.

Café Mocha Latte

1 1/2 cups half-and-half
2 tablespoons brown sugar
2 cups strongly brewed coffee or espresso
1/4 cup chocolate syrup
1 teaspoon vanilla extract
1/4 cup whiskey (optional)

Heat half-and-half in a saucepan over medium-high heat. (Do not boil.) Remove from heat; stir in brown sugar, next 3 ingredients, and, if desired, whiskey. Serve warm or over ice.
Yield: 4 cups latte

Chocolate-Caramel Café au Lait

3/4 cup milk
2 tablespoons caramel-flavored syrup
2 tablespoons chocolate-flavored syrup
1/2 teaspoon vanilla extract
3 cups strongly brewed hot coffee

Combine first 3 ingredients in a small saucepan. Bring to a simmer over medium heat, stirring constantly. Remove from heat; stir in vanilla.
Pour 3/4 cup brewed coffee into each mug. Add 1/4 cup milk mixture to each mug, stirring well. Serve hot.
Yield: 4 cups café au lait

Cappuccino Sipper

1/2 cup sugar
3 cups brewed coffee
3 cups half-and-half
1/4 to 1/2 cup rum
1/4 to 1/2 cup brandy
Sweetened whipped cream
Ground cinnamon (optional)

Bring first 5 ingredients to a boil in a large saucepan over medium heat, stirring constantly. Remove from heat. Top each serving with sweetened whipped cream and, if desired, cinnamon.
Yield: 7 cups sipper

Maple Coffee

2 cups half-and-half (see Note)
3/4 to 1 cup maple syrup (see Note)
3 cups strongly brewed coffee

Cook half-and-half and maple syrup in a saucepan over medium heat until thoroughly heated. (Do not boil.) Stir in coffee.
Yield: 6 cups coffee
Note: To lighten recipe, use fat-free half-and-half, and reduce maple syrup to 2/3 cup.

Low-Carb Christmas

Are you carb-conscious? Spice up your Christmas menu with these mouthwatering alternatives to traditional holiday fare. They're so tasty, they're sure to become year-round favorites!

Holiday guests will savor the zesty flavor of Lemon-Pepper Chicken. Serve it with couscous and steamed snow peas to create a satisfyingly scrumptious meal.

LEMON-PEPPER CHICKEN

Vegetable cooking spray
1 teaspoon olive oil
4 skinned, boned chicken breast halves (4 ounces each)
1 1/4 teaspoons lemon-pepper seasoning
1/4 cup canned reduced-sodium chicken broth
1/4 cup balsamic vinegar

Coat a large nonstick skillet with cooking spray; add oil, and place over medium-high heat until hot. While skillet heats, sprinkle both sides of chicken breasts evenly with lemon-pepper seasoning. Add chicken to skillet, and cook 4 to 5 minutes on each side or until chicken is done. Transfer chicken to a serving platter, and keep warm.

Add broth and vinegar to skillet; cook, stirring constantly, 1 minute or until slightly thickened. Spoon sauce over chicken.

Yield: 4 servings
Note: Serve with couscous and steamed snow peas.
Per Serving: Carbohydrate 0.3g; Calories 138 (18% from fat); Fat 2.7g (sat 0.5g); Protein 26.2g; Fiber 0g; Cholesterol 66mg; Iron 0.9mg; Sodium 233mg; Calcium 13mg

PORT MARINATED STEAKS

Steak marinated in port, a sweet red wine with a bit of brandy added to it, takes on an especially unique flavor. Port has a higher carbohydrate content than dry red wine, but because of its strong flavor, only a small amount is needed. Here, each serving gets about 2 1/2 grams carbohydrate from the port.

1 1/2 pounds lean boneless top sirloin steak
1/2 cup port or sweet red wine
2 tablespoons Worcestershire sauce
2 tablespoons balsamic vinegar
2 cloves garlic, crushed
3 teaspoons dried thyme
Vegetable cooking spray

Trim fat from steak. Combine wine and next 4 ingredients in a heavy-duty, zip-top plastic bag. Add steak; seal bag, and turn bag to coat steak. Marinate in refrigerator 8 hours, turning bag occasionally.

Remove steak from marinade; pour marinade into a small saucepan. Bring marinade to a boil; boil until reduced to 1/4 cup. Set aside.

Coat grill rack with cooking spray; place on grill over medium-hot coals (350° to 400°). Place steak on rack; grill, covered, 5 minutes on each side or to desired degree of doneness. Let steak stand 5 minutes. Cut diagonally across grain into thin slices; drizzle with marinade.

Yield: 6 servings
Per Serving: Carbohydrate 3.6g; Calories 191 (32% from fat); Fat 6.7g (sat 2.6g); Protein 27.9g; Fiber 1.2g; Cholesterol 80mg; Iron 4.6mg; Sodium 111mg; Calcium 53mg

ASIAN MARINATED ASPARAGUS

1 pound asparagus spears
2 tablespoons water
1/4 cup seasoned rice vinegar
2 tablespoons soy sauce
2 teaspoons fresh ginger, chopped
1 teaspoon dark sesame oil

Snap off tough ends of asparagus, and remove scales with a knife or vegetable peeler, if desired. Place asparagus spears and water in a shallow microwave-safe dish. Cover and microwave at HIGH 2 to 4 minutes or until asparagus is crisp-tender; drain. Return asparagus to dish.

Combine vinegar and next 3 ingredients in a small bowl; stir with a whisk until mixture is blended. Pour vinegar mixture over asparagus, turning asparagus to coat. Cover and marinate in refrigerator at least 2 hours, turning asparagus occasionally.

Yield: 4 servings
Per Serving: Carbohydrate 4.9g; Calories 38 (31% from fat); Fat 1.3g (sat 0.2g); Protein 2.5g; Fiber 1.8g; Cholesterol 0mg; Iron 0.9mg; Sodium 518mg; Calcium 20mg

SPINACH FRITTATA

Some marinara sauces are much lower in carbohydrate than others— check the nutrient labels to compare.

2 teaspoons butter
1/2 cup chopped onion
1 garlic clove, minced
1 1/2 cups egg substitute
1/4 teaspoon salt
1/4 teaspoon black pepper
1/8 teaspoon ground nutmeg
1 package (10 ounces) frozen chopped spinach, thawed, drained, and squeezed dry
1/2 cup (2 ounces) shredded Swiss cheese
1 cup warm fat-free marinara sauce

Melt butter in a 10-inch nonstick skillet with sloped sides over medium-high heat. Add onion and garlic; sauté until tender.

Combine egg substitute and next 4 ingredients; add onion mixture, stirring well. Pour egg mixture into skillet. Cover; cook over medium-low heat 10 minutes or until mixture is set. Remove from heat; sprinkle with cheese. Cover; let stand 5 minutes or until cheese melts. Serve with warm marinara sauce.

Yield: 4 servings
Per Serving: Carbohydrate 6.9g; Calories 154 (30% from fat); Fat 5.1g (sat 2.3g); Protein 15.9g; Fiber 3.7g; Cholesterol 10mg; Iron 3.5mg; Sodium 580mg; Calcium 223mg

Make your best showing with this enticing main dish … Port Marinated Steaks. Before grilling, soak sirloin steak for eight hours in a sweet red wine or port to make it tender and tasty. For a delectable side dish, prepare Asian Marinated Asparagus.

Just the right blend of seasonings — garlic, pepper, thyme, salt, lemon juice, and Dijon mustard — gives Mustard-Garlic Lamb Chops its claim to flavor fame. Pair it up with Skillet Zucchini to bring a little taste of summer to your holiday menu.

Mustard-Garlic Lamb Chops

    2   cloves garlic, minced
  ¹/₂   teaspoon freshly ground black pepper
  ¹/₄   teaspoon dried thyme
  ¹/₈   teaspoon salt
    2   teaspoons fresh lemon juice
    2   teaspoons Dijon mustard
    1   teaspoon olive oil
    4   lean lamb loin chops (5 ounces each)
        Vegetable cooking spray

Combine garlic, pepper, thyme, and salt in a small bowl; mash with back of a spoon until mixture forms a paste. Stir in lemon juice, mustard, and olive oil.

Trim fat from chops. Spread garlic mixture over both sides of chops. Place chops on rack of a broiler pan coated with cooking spray. Broil 5¹/₂ inches from heat (with electric oven door partially opened) 6 to 7 minutes on each side or to desired degree of doneness.

Yield: 4 servings

Per Serving: Carbohydrate 1.1g; Calories 192 (44% from fat); Fat 9.3g (sat 3g); Protein 24.3g; Fiber 0.1g; Cholesterol 77mg; Iron 1.8mg; Sodium 216mg; Calcium 21mg

SKILLET ZUCCHINI

    Olive oil-flavored cooking spray
1   teaspoon minced garlic
2   medium zucchini
1/2 teaspoon salt
1/4 teaspoon pepper
1   tablespoon shredded Parmesan cheese

Coat a large nonstick skillet with olive oil-flavored cooking spray, and place over medium heat. Add minced garlic, and sauté 1 minute. Add zucchini, sliced and halved; sprinkle with salt and pepper. Cook until zucchini is tender, stirring occasionally. Sprinkle with Parmesan cheese.

Yield: 4 servings (serving size: 1/2 cup)
Per Serving: Carbohydrate 2.3g; Calories 16 (28% from fat); Fat 0.5g (sat 0.3g); Protein 1.3g; Fiber 0.3g; Cholesterol 1mg; Iron 0.5mg; Sodium 318mg; Calcium 38mg

SOUTHWESTERN GRILLED FLANK STEAK

A homemade spice mix takes just a minute or two to assemble and gives flank steak a real flavor boost.

1   lean flank steak (1 1/2 pounds, about 3/4-inch thick)
2   tablespoons Hungarian sweet paprika
1   tablespoon chili powder
2   teaspoons ground cumin
1   teaspoon ground cinnamon
1/2 teaspoon salt
    Vegetable cooking spray

Trim excess fat from steak. Combine paprika and next 4 ingredients; rub over both sides of steak. Place steak in a dish; cover and marinate in refrigerator at least 4 hours.

Prepare grill. Place steak on grill rack coated with cooking spray; cover and grill 4 minutes on each side or until desired degree of doneness. Remove steak from grill; let stand 5 minutes before slicing. Cut steak diagonally across the grain into thin slices.

Yield: 6 servings (serving size: 3 ounces)
Per Serving: Carbohydrate 2.6g; Calories 271 (55% from fat); Fat 16.5g (sat 6.9g); Protein 27.5g; Fiber 1.1g; Cholesterol 74mg; Iron 4mg; Sodium 298mg; Calcium 25mg

CONFETTI CHEESE OMELET

Great for breakfast but hearty enough for dinner, omelets are an easy option any night of the week.

    Vegetable cooking spray
1/4 cup chopped red bell pepper
1/4 cup chopped green or orange bell pepper
1/4 cup sliced green onions
1   cup egg substitute
1/4 teaspoon salt
1/4 teaspoon freshly ground black pepper
1/2 cup (2 ounces) shredded reduced-fat Cheddar cheese

Heat a 10-inch nonstick skillet coated with cooking spray over medium heat. Add peppers and green onions; cook 4 minutes, stirring occasionally.

Pour egg substitute into skillet; sprinkle with salt and pepper. Cook, without stirring, 2 to 3 minutes or until golden brown on bottom. Sprinkle with cheese. Loosen omelet with a spatula; fold in half. Cook 2 additional minutes or until egg mixture is set and cheese begins to melt. Slide omelet onto a plate; cut in half.

Yield: 2 servings (serving size: 1/2 omelet)
Per Serving: Carbohydrate 6.5g; Calories 165 (34% from fat); Fat 6.1g (sat 4g); Protein 20g; Fiber 1.1g; Cholesterol 20mg; Iron 2.3mg; Sodium 786mg; Calcium 254mg

BALSAMIC PORK CHOPS

4   boneless center-cut pork loin chops (4 ounces each, cut 1/2-inch thick)
1   teaspoon salt-free lemon-herb seasoning
    Vegetable cooking spray
1/2 cup balsamic vinegar
1/3 cup fat-free, reduced-sodium chicken broth

Trim fat from chops. Sprinkle chops evenly on both sides with seasoning. Coat a medium nonstick skillet with cooking spray; place over medium-high heat until hot. Add chops, and cook 3 to 4 minutes on each side or until lightly browned. Remove chops from skillet, and keep warm.

Wipe drippings from skillet with a paper towel. Combine vinegar and broth in skillet. Cook over medium-high heat until mixture is reduced to a thin sauce (about 5 to 6 minutes), stirring occasionally. Spoon sauce over chops.

Yield: 4 servings
Per Serving: Carbohydrate 0.9g; Calories 210 (49% from fat); Fat 11.4g (sat 3.8g); Protein 24.3g; Fiber 0.1g; Cholesterol 77mg; Iron 1.1mg; Sodium 178mg; Calcium 31mg

NEIGHBORHOOD
Round Robin

The season of "Ho! Ho! Ho!" finds many of us on the "Go! Go! Go!" As a result, our Christmas wish lists often include a home-cooked meal that we don't have to prepare ourselves. The solution? … get together with three friends and plan a round robin! We've included four menus that will each serve four families of four. Each family takes their turn cooking for one evening, making dinner for all four families in the group. So by cooking one meal, you'll get three in return! Remember to deliver the meals in disposable containers, so no one has to do the dishes.

Our hearty Chicken Tetrazzini and Cheese Twists will satisfy hungry appetites. For a refreshing change from canned green beans, try our lively Green Bean, Walnut, and Feta Salad.

MENU 1 — Tempting Tetrazzini Meal

GREEN BEAN, WALNUT, AND FETA SALAD

- 4 pounds fresh green beans, trimmed
- 2 small purple onions, thinly sliced
- 2 packages (4 ounces each) crumbled feta cheese
- 2 cups coarsely chopped walnuts or pecans, toasted
- 1½ cups olive oil
- ½ cup white wine vinegar
- 2 tablespoons chopped fresh dill
- 1 teaspoon minced garlic
- ½ teaspoon salt
- ½ teaspoon pepper

Cut green beans into thirds, and arrange in a steamer basket over boiling water. Cover and steam 15 minutes or until crisp-tender. Immediately plunge into cold water to stop the cooking process; drain and pat dry.

Toss together green beans, onion, cheese, and walnuts in a large bowl. Cover and chill 1 hour.

Whisk together olive oil and next 5 ingredients; cover and chill 1 hour.

Pour vinaigrette over green bean mixture, and chill 1 hour; toss just before serving.

Yield: 16 servings

CHICKEN TETRAZZINI

- 1 cup butter or margarine
- 1 medium-size sweet onion, diced
- 1 cup all-purpose flour
- 8 cups milk
- 1 cup dry white wine or chicken broth
- 4 tablespoons chicken bouillon granules
- 2 teaspoons seasoned pepper
- 3 cups freshly grated Parmesan cheese, divided
- 8 cups diced cooked chicken
- 23 ounces vermicelli, cooked
- 2 jars (6 ounces each) sliced mushrooms, drained
- 2 cups soft breadcrumbs
- 4 tablespoons butter or margarine, melted

Melt 1 cup butter in a Dutch oven over medium-high heat; add onion, and sauté 5 minutes or until tender.

Whisk in flour until smooth, and cook, whisking constantly, 1 minute. Gradually add milk and wine; cook, whisking constantly, 5 to 6 minutes or until thickened.

Add bouillon granules, seasoned pepper, and 2 cups cheese. Cook, whisking constantly, 1 minute or until bouillon granules dissolve and cheese melts. Remove from heat. Stir in chicken, pasta, and mushrooms. Spoon into 4 lightly greased 1½ to 2-quart disposable pans. Chill until ready to bake.

Bake chicken mixture, covered, at 350° for 20 minutes.

Stir together remaining 1 cup cheese, breadcrumbs, and 4 tablespoons melted butter, and sprinkle evenly over casseroles. Bake casseroles 10 to 15 more minutes or until golden.

Yield: 16 servings

Note: To reheat casseroles, let stand at room temperature 20 minutes. Bake, covered, at 350° for 15 minutes. Uncover and bake 10 minutes or until thoroughly heated.

CHEESE TWISTS

Recast puff pastry sheets into flaky spiral appetizers seasoned with Parmesan cheese and pepper.

- ½ cup grated Parmesan cheese
- ¾ teaspoon seasoned pepper
- ½ teaspoon dried parsley flakes
- ¼ teaspoon garlic powder
- 1 package (17.3 ounces) frozen puff pastry sheets, thawed
- 1 egg white, lightly beaten

Combine first 4 ingredients in a small bowl; stir well and set aside.

Unfold one puff pastry sheet. Brush lightly with egg white. Sprinkle 2 tablespoons cheese mixture evenly over surface of pastry sheet; lightly press cheese mixture into pastry sheet. Turn pastry sheet over and repeat procedure.

Cut pastry sheet in half; cut each half into 9 strips (about 1" wide). Gently twist each strip into a tight spiral and place on lightly greased baking sheets.

Repeat procedure with remaining pastry sheet, egg white, and cheese mixture. Bake at 350° for 18 to 20 minutes or until golden.

Yield: 3 dozen twists

PECAN-RAISIN TARTS

- 2 cups sugar
- ½ cup butter or margarine, melted
- 4 large eggs, lightly beaten
- 2 tablespoons white vinegar
- 1 teaspoon ground cinnamon
- 1 teaspoon ground nutmeg
- 2 cups golden raisins
- 2 cups chopped pecans, toasted
- 2½ packages (10 ounces each) frozen tart shells, thawed
- Garnishes: whipped cream, ground nutmeg

Stir together first 6 ingredients in a large bowl. Stir in raisins and toasted pecans.

Spoon filling evenly into tart shells. Place tarts on a large baking sheet.

Bake at 325° for 40 to 43 minutes or until golden. Garnish, if desired.

Yield: 20 servings

These **Pecan-Raisin Tarts** may be small in size, but they're big on flavor! The mini pecan pies are packed with golden raisins for an added punch.

MENU 2 — Home-Cooked Calzone Meal

CHILLED VEGETABLE SALAD

- 1 cup sugar
- ³/₄ cup cider vinegar
- ¹/₂ cup vegetable oil
- 1 medium-size green bell pepper, chopped
- 1 medium onion, chopped
- 3 celery ribs, sliced
- 1 jar (7 ounces) diced pimiento, undrained
- 1 can (15¹/₄ ounces) small sweet green peas, drained
- 1 can (14¹/₂ ounces) French-cut green beans, drained
- 1 can (11 ounces) white shoepeg corn, drained
- ¹/₂ teaspoon salt
- ¹/₄ teaspoon pepper

Bring first 3 ingredients to a boil in small saucepan over medium heat; cook, stirring often, 5 minutes or until sugar dissolves. Remove dressing from heat, and cool 30 minutes.

Stir together bell pepper and next 8 ingredients in a large bowl; gently stir in dressing. Cover and chill salad for 8 hours. Serve with a slotted spoon.

Yield: 8 cups salad

Note: Salad may be stored in an airtight container in the refrigerator for several days.

EASY CHEESY CALZONES

- 1 container (15 ounces) ricotta cheese
- 1 cup (4 ounces) shredded provolone cheese
- 1 cup (4 ounces) shredded Parmesan cheese
- ¹/₂ cup chopped fresh basil
- 2 garlic cloves, pressed
- ¹/₂ teaspoon salt
- ¹/₂ teaspoon pepper
- 2 cans (10.2 ounces each) refrigerated jumbo biscuits
- 1 large egg
- 1 tablespoon water
- 1 can (14¹/₂ ounces) diced tomatoes, drained

Stir together first 7 ingredients. Split biscuits in half; roll each half into a 4-inch circle on a lightly floured surface.

Whisk together egg and 1 tablespoon water in a small bowl until blended.

Spoon ricotta mixture evenly onto each circle, leaving a 1-inch border. Top evenly with tomato. Brush edges lightly with water. Fold dough over filling. Press edges with a fork to seal; prick tops. Brush calzones with egg mixture. Place on lightly greased baking sheets.

Bake at 450° for 6 to 8 minutes or until golden brown. (Do not overbake.) Serve immediately.

Yield: 20 servings

A blend of three cheeses — ricotta, provolone, and Parmesan — gives **Easy Cheesy Calzones** a taste that will have them going, going, gone. **Chilled Vegetable Salad**, which can be made ahead of time and stored in the refrigerator, tastes as festive as it looks.

Want a little sweet indulgence? Try our Layered Brownies. What makes this recipe so irresistible is that it calls for topping the brownies with layers of **Vanilla Cream Topping** and Brownie Glaze. Yum!

LAYERED BROWNIES

The Vanilla Cream Topping and Brownie Glaze add extra layers of texture and sweetness to this recipe.

- 4 unsweetened chocolate baking squares (1 ounce each)
- 1 cup butter or margarine
- 2 cups sugar
- 4 large eggs, lightly beaten
- 1 cup all-purpose flour
- 1 cup chopped pecans, toasted
  Vanilla Cream Topping
  Brownie Glaze

Microwave chocolate and butter in a 2-quart glass bowl at HIGH 1 1/2 minutes or until melted, stirring twice. Add sugar and eggs, stirring until blended. Stir in flour and chopped pecans. Pour into a lightly greased, aluminum foil-lined 13 x 9-inch pan.

Bake at 350° for 20 to 23 minutes. Cool on a wire rack 1 hour.

Spread cooled brownies with Vanilla Cream Topping; chill 45 minutes. Pour Brownie Glaze over Vanilla Cream Topping, and spread evenly. Chill 1 hour. Let stand at room temperature 15 minutes; cut into 1-inch squares.
Yield: 48 squares

VANILLA CREAM TOPPING

- 1 cup butter, melted
- 1 package (16 ounces) powdered sugar
- 1/4 cup half-and-half
- 2 teaspoons vanilla extract

Stir together butter, sugar, half-and-half, and vanilla until smooth.

BROWNIE GLAZE

- 4 semisweet chocolate baking squares (1 ounce each)
- 1/4 cup butter

Microwave chocolate squares and butter in a 1-quart glass bowl at HIGH 1 1/2 minutes or until melted, stirring twice.

Placed on a bed of spinach and cream cheese and topped with tomato slices and Parmesan cheese, **Chicken Italiano** is a mouth-watering main dish. Present it with **Marinated Asparagus** and Easy Italian Bread for a meal that will have recipients saying, "Mama, mia!"

MENU 3 — Irresistible Chicken Italiano Meal

EASY ITALIAN BREAD

  3 frozen bread dough loaves (1 pound each), thawed
  3 tablespoons olive oil
  1 tablespoon Italian seasoning
  ³/₄ teaspoon garlic powder
  ¹/₂ cup shredded Parmesan cheese

Divide each bread dough loaf into 3 equal portions. Roll each portion into a 6¹/₂-inch circle, and place on a lightly greased baking sheets. Brush with olive oil, and sprinkle with Italian seasoning, garlic powder, and Parmesan cheese.

Bake at 375° for 10 minutes. Prick several times with a fork. Bake 8 to 10 more minutes or until golden. Cool slightly on baking sheets. Cut each round into 4 wedges. Brush with additional olive oil.
Yield: 16 servings

MARINATED ASPARAGUS

  4 pounds fresh asparagus
  1¹/₂ cups olive oil
  2 tablespoons sugar
  1 cup white balsamic vinegar
  8 garlic cloves, minced
  2 teaspoons red pepper flakes

Snap off tough ends of asparagus, and cook asparagus in boiling water to cover 3 minutes or until asparagus is crisp-tender; drain.

Plunge asparagus into ice water to stop the cooking process; drain. Arrange asparagus in two 13 x 9-inch baking dishes.

Whisk together olive oil, sugar, balsamic vinegar, garlic, and red pepper flakes until well blended; pour over asparagus. Cover and chill 8 hours. Drain before placing in containers to transport.
Yield: 16 servings

CHICKEN ITALIANO

8 packages (10 ounces each) frozen chopped spinach, thawed and drained
4 packages (8 ounces each) cream cheese, softened
   Vegetable cooking spray
3 cups Italian-seasoned breadcrumbs
16 skinned, boned chicken breasts (4 ounces each), partially frozen (see Note)
2 tablespoons olive oil
16 slices (1 ounce each) mozzarella cheese , cut in half
1 teaspoon dried oregano
32 slices tomato (8 medium tomatoes, sliced ½-inch thick each)
1 cup grated fresh Parmesan cheese

Combine spinach and cream cheese. Press spinach mixture evenly into bottoms of four 13 x 9-inch disposable baking pans coated with cooking spray.

Place breadcrumbs in a shallow dish. Cut each chicken breast in half horizontally to make 2 cutlets. Dredge chicken in breadcrumbs.

Heat oil in a large nonstick skillet over medium-high heat. Cook chicken in batches 2 minutes on each side or until browned, adding additional oil as needed. Arrange chicken evenly over spinach mixture. Top with mozzarella, and sprinkle with oregano. Top with the tomato slices and Parmesan. Cover and chill up to 24 hours, if desired.

To bake, let chicken stand at room temperature 20 minutes. Bake, uncovered, at 350° for 30 minutes or until thoroughly heated.

Yield: 16 servings
Note: Partially freeze chicken for easier slicing.

GINGERED AMBROSIA

12 large navel oranges
4 cans (20 ounces each) pineapple chunks, drained
1⅓ cups sweetened flaked coconut
½ cup fresh mint leaves, cut into strips
¼ cup plus 1 tablespoon fresh lime juice
3 tablespoons grated fresh ginger
   Garnish: chopped fresh mint leaves

Peel and section oranges over a bowl, reserving juice. Combine orange sections, juice, and remaining ingredients; gently toss. Cover and chill until ready to serve. Garnish, if desired.

Yield: 16 servings

When you have Gingered Ambrosia as the dessert, you'll be able to imagine yourself on a warm exotic island, no matter how cold it is outside. The tropical blend of oranges, pineapple, and coconut gets just the right zip from mint, lime juice, and ginger.

MENU 4 — Simply Sensational Lasagna Meal

CHOCOLATE-CHESTNUT PASTRIES

  2 packages (10 ounces each) frozen puff pastry shells, thawed
  1 pound whole chestnuts, shelled (about 2²/₃ cups nut meat)
  2 cups sugar
  2 cups milk
  2 semisweet chocolate baking bars (4 ounces each), coarsely chopped
  ¹/₄ cup rum or brandy or 2 teaspoons rum flavoring
  2¹/₂ cups whipping cream
    Garnishes: chocolate shavings, chocolate syrup

Prepare pastry shells according to package directions; set aside.

Bring chestnuts, sugar, and milk to a boil in a small saucepan, stirring until sugar dissolves; reduce heat, and simmer 30 minutes or until chestnuts are tender and mixture thickens.

Microwave chocolate in a glass bowl at HIGH 30 seconds to 1 minute or until melted, stirring once.

Remove chestnut mixture from heat. Stir in melted chocolate and rum.

Process chestnut mixture, in batches, in a food processor until smooth, stopping to scrape down sides. Cool completely.

Beat cream at medium speed with an electric mixer until soft peaks form. Gently fold whipped cream into chestnut mixture. (Mixture will be soft.) Cover and chill at least 1 hour or overnight.

Spoon mixture into prepared pastry shells. Garnish, if desired.
Yield: 16 servings

SEASONED BREADSTICKS

  1 can (11 ounces) refrigerated breadsticks
    Olive oil
  1 teaspoon chili powder
  ¹/₂ teaspoon ground cumin

Let dough sit at room temperature 30 minutes. Unroll dough onto a large cutting board. Dough will be perforated; separate at perforations. Cut each dough section in half crosswise. Separate dough into 24 pieces; stretch each piece to 10 inches, and place ¹/₄ inch apart on cutting board. Brush dough lightly with olive oil.

Combine chili powder and cumin; sprinkle evenly over dough. Twist ends of dough pieces in opposite directions 3 or 4 times. Place breadsticks 1 inch apart on ungreased baking sheets, pressing ends securely.

Bake at 350° for 12 to 14 minutes or until golden. Transfer to wire racks to cool.
Yield: 2 dozen breadsticks

APPLE-SPINACH SALAD

  6 Granny Smith apples, coarsely chopped
  ¹/₄ cup orange juice
  6 packages (6 ounces each) fresh baby spinach (see Note)
  1¹/₂ cups salted cashews
  ³/₄ cup raisins or golden raisins
  ³/₄ cup sugar
  ³/₄ cup vegetable oil
  ¹/₄ cup plus 2 tablespoons balsamic or apple cider vinegar
  ³/₄ teaspoon celery salt

Toss chopped apples with orange juice; drain. Combine one-fourth of apples and one-fourth each of spinach, cashews, and raisins in 4 large zip-top plastic bags.

Whisk together sugar and next 3 ingredients until well blended. Pour into 4 small jars. Cover and chill salad and dressing until ready to transport. Toss salad and dressing just before serving.
Yield: 16 servings
Note: Three 10-ounce packages regular spinach may be substituted.

EXTRA-EASY LASAGNA

  4 pounds ground sirloin
  16 cups tomato-basil pasta sauce
  24 uncooked lasagna noodles
  4 containers (15 ounces each) ricotta cheese
  10 cups shredded mozzarella cheese
  1 cup hot water

Cook sirloin in a large skillet over medium heat, stirring until it crumbles and is no longer pink; drain. Stir in pasta sauce.

Spread one-third of meat sauce evenly in 4 lightly greased 11 x 7-inch disposable pans; layer each pan with 3 uncooked noodles. Spread one-half each of ricotta cheese and mozzarella cheese evenly over the 4 pans of noodles. (The ricotta cheese layers will be thin.) Repeat procedure; spread remaining one-third of meat sauce over mozzarella cheese. Slowly pour ¹/₄ cup hot water around inside edge of each pan. Tightly cover pans with 2 layers of heavy-duty aluminum foil. Chill until ready to bake.

Let lasagna stand at room temperature 20 minutes. Bake, covered, at 375° for 45 minutes; uncover and bake 10 more minutes. Let stand 10 minutes before serving.
Yield: 24 servings

Our version of **Extra-Easy Lasagna** is so deliciously simple, you'll love it all the more! Apple-Spinach Salad makes a colorful side dish. And who can eat lasagna without some **Seasoned Breadsticks**? Just remember to save a little room for some Chocolate-Chestnut Pastries (not shown).

Sweet Sensations

You can satisfy even the most avid sweet tooth with this collection of confections! From cakes and cookies to pie and pudding, there's a sweet temptation for every taste.

Take traditional pecan pie to the next level of holiday indulgence by making Pecan Pie Cake instead. Layered with Pecan Pie Filling, this cake tastes as good as it looks.

PECAN PIE CAKE

- 3 cups finely chopped pecans, toasted and divided
- ¹/₂ cup butter or margarine, softened
- ¹/₂ cup shortening
- 2 cups sugar
- 5 large eggs, separated
- 1 tablespoon vanilla extract
- 2 cups all-purpose flour
- 1 teaspoon baking soda
- 1 cup buttermilk
- ³/₄ cup dark corn syrup
- 1 recipe Pecan Pie Filling

Sprinkle 2 cups pecans evenly into 3 generously buttered 9-inch round cake pans; shake to coat bottoms and sides of pans.

Beat butter and shortening at medium speed with an electric mixer until fluffy; gradually add sugar, beating well. Add egg yolks, 1 at a time, beating until blended after each addition. Stir in vanilla.

Add flour and baking soda to butter mixture alternately with buttermilk, beginning and ending with flour. Beat at low speed until blended after each addition. Stir in remaining 1 cup pecans.

Beat egg whites at medium speed until stiff peaks form; fold one-third of egg whites into batter. Fold in remaining egg whites. (Do not overmix.) Pour batter into prepared pans.

Bake at 350° for 23 to 25 minutes or until done. Cool in pans on wire racks 10 minutes. Invert layers onto wax paper-lined wire racks. Brush tops and sides of layers with corn syrup, and cool completely.

Spread half of Pecan Pie Filling on 1 layer, pecan side up. Place second layer, pecan side up, on filling; spread with remaining filling. Top with remaining layer, pecan side up.
Yield: one 3-layer cake

PECAN PIE FILLING

- ¹/₂ cup firmly packed dark brown sugar
- ³/₄ cup dark corn syrup
- ¹/₃ cup cornstarch
- 4 egg yolks
- 1¹/₂ cups half-and-half
- ¹/₈ teaspoon salt
- 3 tablespoons butter or margarine
- 1 teaspoon vanilla extract

Whisk together first 6 ingredients in a heavy 3-quart saucepan until smooth. Bring mixture to a boil over medium heat, whisking constantly; boil 1 minute or until thickened. Remove from heat; whisk in butter and vanilla. Place a sheet of wax paper directly on surface of mixture to prevent a film from forming, and chill 4 hours.
Yield: about 3 cups filling
Note: To chill filling quickly, pour filling into a bowl. Place bowl in a larger bowl filled with ice. Whisk constantly until cool (about 15 minutes).

PEANUT BUTTER CRUNCH CANDY
This candy will remind you of a famous candy bar.

- 1 cup creamy peanut butter
- 1 cup sugar
- ¹/₃ cup water
- ¹/₃ cup light corn syrup
- 1 package (12 ounces) semisweet chocolate morsels, melted

Butter an 8-inch square pan.

Heat peanut butter in top of a double boiler or on low heat in a medium saucepan, stirring constantly, until softened; set aside.

Combine sugar, water, and syrup in a small saucepan. Cook over medium heat, stirring constantly, until sugar is dissolved. Cover and cook 2 to 3 minutes to wash crystals from sides of pan. Uncover and cook, without stirring, to 310° (hard-crack stage), about 16 minutes.

Working quickly, pour syrup mixture immediately into peanut butter, stirring constantly, just until blended. Pour into prepared pan. Let cool 1 minute. Score (cut through but not to bottom of pan) into 36 squares. Cool completely.

Cut candy with a sharp knife along scored lines. Dip candy in melted chocolate, allowing excess chocolate to drip back into pan. Cool completely on wax paper.
Yield: 1 pound (36 pieces) candy

If you're looking for a delectable treat for parties or gift giving, **Peanut Butter Crunch Candy** is ideal. The homemade mini candy bars are sure to delight the chocoholics on your list.

A chorus of spices gives this Pumpkin Cake a flavor that will have taste buds singing for joy.

PUMPKIN CAKE

CAKE

- 3 cups sugar
- 1 cup shortening
- 3 large eggs
- 2 cups mashed cooked pumpkin
- 3 cups all-purpose flour
- 1 teaspoon baking powder
- 1/2 teaspoon baking soda
- 1/4 teaspoon salt
- 1/4 teaspoon ground cinnamon
- 1/4 teaspoon ground cloves
- 1/4 teaspoon ground allspice
- 1/4 teaspoon ground nutmeg
- 1 teaspoon vanilla extract
- 1 cup chopped pecans, toasted

GLAZE

- 2 cups powdered sugar
- 3 to 3 1/2 tablespoons milk
- 1 teaspoon vanilla extract

For cake, beat sugar and shortening at medium speed with an electric mixer until creamy. Add eggs and pumpkin, beating until blended. Combine flour and next 7 ingredients; gradually add to pumpkin mixture, beating until blended. Stir in vanilla and pecans. Pour into a greased and floured 10-inch tube pan.

Bake at 350° for 10 minutes. Reduce temperature to 300°; bake 1 hour and 33 to 35 minutes, or until a wooden pick inserted in center of cake comes out clean.

For glaze, combine all ingredients; stir until smooth. Drizzle glaze over cooled cake.
Yield: one 10-inch cake

UPSIDE-DOWN APPLE TART

- 1/4 cup butter or margarine
- 1/2 cup firmly packed light brown sugar
- 3 cups Granny Smith apple slices
- 2 tablespoons brandy or orange liqueur
- 2 teaspoons lemon juice
- 1/2 teaspoon ground cinnamon
- 1/4 teaspoon ground nutmeg
- 1/2 (17.3-ounce) package frozen puff pastry sheets, thawed
  Whipped cream (optional)

Melt butter in a 10-inch ovenproof skillet; add sugar, and cook, stirring constantly, over medium heat 3 minutes or until bubbly. Remove from heat and cool slightly.

Arrange apple slices over sugar mixture. Drizzle apple slices with brandy and lemon juice, and sprinkle with cinnamon and nutmeg.

Roll pastry sheet into an 11-inch square; cut a 10-inch circle from pastry square. Remove and discard trimmings. Place circle over apples (do not seal pastry to skillet).

Bake at 400° for 20 minutes or until golden. Remove from oven, and cool 2 minutes. Invert onto a serving dish, and serve with whipped cream, if desired.
Yield: 6 servings

CRANBERRY STREUSEL PIE

- 1/2 (15-ounce) package refrigerated piecrusts
- 4 cups fresh or frozen cranberries
- 1/2 cup granulated sugar
- 1/2 cup firmly packed light brown sugar
- 1 cup chopped walnuts
- 1 teaspoon ground cinnamon
- 2 large eggs
- 1/2 cup butter or margarine, melted
- 2/3 cup sugar
- 1/4 cup plus 2 tablespoons all-purpose flour

Press piecrust into a 9-inch deep dish pie plate according to package directions; fold edges under and crimp.

Stir together cranberries and next 4 ingredients; spoon into piecrust.

Whisk together eggs and remaining ingredients, and pour over cranberry mixture.

Bake at 400° for 20 minutes. Reduce temperature to 350° and bake 25 minutes or until set, shielding crust during the last 15 minutes of baking.

Yield: one 9-inch pie

Lemon-Swirled Gingerbread (*above*) gets its zing from a blend of cream cheese, sugar, and lemon curd baked between layers of gingerbread. A flavor sensation, Cranberry Streusel Pie (*below*) is loaded with juicy cranberries and crunchy walnuts.

LEMON-SWIRLED GINGERBREAD

The traditional pairing of gingerbread and lemon curd takes a surprising turn in this recipe—the lemon curd is baked right in.

    2 packages (3 ounces each) cream cheese,
         softened
  1/4 cup sugar
    1 large egg
  1/2 cup lemon curd
    1 package (14.5 ounces) gingerbread mix
         Garnish: lemon curls (see Note)

Place cream cheese in a medium mixing bowl; beat at medium speed with an electric mixer until smooth. Gradually add 1/4 cup sugar, beating well. Add egg, beating just until blended. Fold in lemon curd.

Prepare gingerbread batter according to package directions. Pour half of batter into a greased 8-inch square pan. Dollop lemon mixture over batter; pour remaining batter over lemon mixture. Swirl a knife through batter, touching bottom of pan and swirling to bring some lemon mixture to top of cake. Bake at 350° for 35 to 37 minutes or until knife inserted in center comes out clean. Cool in pan on a wire rack. Cut into squares; garnish each with a lemon curl.

Yield: 9 servings

Note: For lemon curl garnish, use a citrus peeler or knife to peel strips of rind from a lemon, leaving white pith on fruit. Cut rind into long, thin strips. Wrap strips tightly around a pencil to create curls. Freeze briefly; then remove strips from pencil.

CRANBERRY CHRISTMAS TREE BREAD

With its festive presentation, this easy roll recipe is a sweet treat for parties, snacks, or breakfast. Frozen bread dough and purchased frosting make it easy enough to prepare anytime.

  1 1/2 cups fresh or frozen cranberries
    3/4 cup sugar
      1 tablespoon fresh orange juice
  1 1/2 teaspoons grated orange rind
    1/2 (32-ounce) package frozen bread dough, thawed
      2 tablespoons butter, melted
    1/3 cup chopped walnuts (optional)
    1/4 cup cream cheese-flavored ready-made frosting

Combine first 4 ingredients in a medium saucepan, stirring well. (Frozen berries do not have to thaw first.) Cook over medium-high heat, stirring constantly, until thickened (about 10 minutes). Set aside, and cool.

Roll dough on a lightly floured surface into a 9 x 18-inch rectangle; brush with melted butter. Spread cranberry mixture over dough to within 1/2 inch of edges. Sprinkle with walnuts, if desired. Roll up dough, starting at one long side, pressing gently to contain filling; pinch ends to seal. Cut roll into 16 equal slices (about 1 1/8-inch thick).

On lower third of a large greased baking sheet, arrange 5 slices, cut sides up, in a row with edges touching. Form tree with additional rows of rolls, ending with 1 roll on top of tree and 1 roll on bottom for trunk.

Cover and let rise in a warm place (85°), free from drafts, 30 to 45 minutes or until doubled in bulk. Bake at 350° for 20 to 25 minutes or until lightly browned. Carefully remove from baking sheet, and cool on a wire rack.

Place frosting in a 2-cup glass measuring cup. Microwave, uncovered, at HIGH for 20 to 25 seconds or until drizzling consistency; drizzle over bread.

Yield: 16 servings

O Christmas tree, O Christmas tree, how tasty are your branches! Sweetly "trimmed" in ready-made frosting, Cranberry Christmas Tree Bread is a simply scrumptious selection for your holiday breakfast.

Eggnog is a time-honored holiday treat. Now you can treat family and friends to even more flavorful fun with temptingly rich **Eggnog Truffles**!

EGGNOG TRUFFLES

The freezing steps are worth it for the delicious results you get with these truffles. They're better than drinking homemade eggnog.

  8 squares (1 ounce each) premium white chocolate
¹/₂ cup sifted powdered sugar
¹/₄ cup butter, softened
¹/₄ cup refrigerated eggnog
  2 tablespoons dark rum
¹/₄ teaspoon ground nutmeg
³/₄ cup finely chopped pecans, toasted
  8 ounces vanilla-flavored candy coating, melted

Melt white chocolate according to package directions. Add powdered sugar, butter, and eggnog; stir gently until mixture is smooth. Add rum and nutmeg, stirring just until blended. Cover and freeze at least 2 hours.

Let truffle mixture stand at room temperature 1 to 2 minutes to soften, if necessary. Using 2 small spoons, shape mixture into 1-inch balls. Quickly roll in pecans. Place on a wax paper-lined jellyroll pan; cover and freeze until firm.

Remove truffles from freezer; reshape into balls, if necessary. Using two forks, quickly dip each truffle into melted coating. Place on wax paper to harden. Store truffles in freezer up to one week.
Yield: 2 dozen truffles

BLACK WALNUT PIE

  6 large eggs
²/₃ cup firmly packed brown sugar
  2 cups maple syrup
  2 teaspoons grated lemon rind
  2 teaspoons fresh lemon juice
  1 teaspoon vanilla extract
¹/₄ teaspoon salt
¹/₄ cup plus 2 tablespoons butter, softened
  2 cups black walnut pieces, toasted
  1 unbaked 9-inch pastry shell
    Sweetened whipped cream

Beat eggs and sugar at medium speed with an electric mixer until smooth. Add syrup and next 5 ingredients, beating until smooth.

Place walnuts in pastry shell; pour filling over nuts.

Bake at 375° for 35 minutes (center of pie will not be set). Cool completely and serve with whipped cream.
Yield: one 9-inch pie

UPSIDE-DOWN DATE PUDDING

    1 cup whole pitted dates, chopped
    1 cup boiling water
  ¹/₂ cup granulated sugar
    2 cups firmly packed brown sugar, divided
    3 tablespoons butter, divided
    1 large egg
1 ¹/₂ cups all-purpose flour
    1 teaspoon baking soda
  ¹/₂ teaspoon baking powder
  ¹/₂ teaspoon salt
    1 cup chopped walnuts
1 ¹/₂ cups boiling water
      Sweetened whipped cream

Combine dates and 1 cup boiling water in a small bowl; set aside.

Combine granulated sugar, ¹/₂ cup brown sugar, 2 tablespoons butter, and egg in a large mixing bowl; beat at medium speed with an electric mixer until blended.

Combine flour and next 3 ingredients; stir well. Add to sugar mixture, beating well. (Mixture will be crumbly.) Stir in nuts and cooled date mixture.

Spoon batter into a lightly greased 9 x 13-inch pan. Combine remaining 1¹/₂ cups brown sugar, 1¹/₂ cups boiling water, and remaining 1 tablespoon butter, stirring mixture well.

Pour brown sugar mixture evenly over batter. Bake at 375° for 35 to 40 minutes. Serve warm with whipped cream.
Yield: 12 servings

CHERRY COBBLER

3 cans (14.5 ounces each) pitted tart red
   cherries (see Note)
1 1/2 cups sugar, divided
3 tablespoons cornstarch
1/2 teaspoon red liquid food coloring (optional)
3 tablespoons butter or margarine
1 tablespoon grated lemon rind
1/4 teaspoon almond extract
1 cup all-purpose flour
1 teaspoon baking powder
1/2 teaspoon salt
1/2 cup milk
1/4 cup butter or margarine, softened
1 teaspoon vanilla extract
1 large egg
   Ice cream

Drain cherries, reserving 1/2 cup juice. Bring cherries,
reserved juice, 3/4 cup sugar, cornstarch, and, if desired,
food coloring to a boil in a medium saucepan, stirring
constantly. Boil, stirring constantly, 1 minute. Remove from
heat; stir in 3 tablespoons butter, lemon rind, and almond
extract. Pour into a lightly greased 7 x 11-inch baking dish.

Combine remaining 3/4 cup sugar, flour, baking powder,
and salt in a large mixing bowl. Add milk, 1/4 cup butter,
and vanilla, and beat at medium speed with an electric
mixer 2 minutes. Add egg, and beat 2 more minutes. Spoon
batter evenly over cherry mixture.

Bake at 350° for 40 to 45 minutes or until golden,
shielding with aluminum foil during the last 10 minutes to
prevent excessive browning, if necessary. Cool in dish on a
wire rack 15 to 20 minutes. Serve warm with ice cream.
Yield: 6 servings
Note: Six cups pitted fresh cherries (about 2 1/2 pounds) can
be substituted. Substitute 1/2 cup water for reserved juice.

ULTIMATE CHOCOLATE COMFORT COOKIES

*Chock-full of all your favorites—chocolate chips, pecans, even
marshmallow—these cookies offer something to everyone!*

1 cup unsalted butter, softened
1 package (3 ounces) cream cheese, softened
1 cup sugar
1 large egg
2 squares (1 ounce each) unsweetened chocolate,
   melted and cooled
2 tablespoons milk
1 1/2 teaspoons vanilla extract
2 cups plus 2 tablespoons all-purpose flour
1/2 teaspoon baking powder
1/2 teaspoon salt
1/4 cup Dutch process cocoa or regular cocoa
1 cup marshmallow cream
1 cup chopped pecans
1 package (11 ounces) semisweet chocolate mega-
   morsels or white chocolate morsels (2 cups)
1/2 cup sweetened dried cranberries

Beat butter and cream cheese at medium speed with an
electric mixer until creamy; gradually add sugar, beating
well. Add egg, beating well. Add melted chocolate, milk,
and vanilla; beat well.

Combine flour and next 3 ingredients; add to butter
mixture, beating well. Stir in marshmallow cream and
remaining ingredients, mixing well.

Drop dough by heaping tablespoonfuls onto lightly
greased cookie sheets. Bake at 325° for 13 minutes or until
done. Cool 1 minute on cookie sheets; remove to wire
racks and cool completely.
Yield: 4 dozen cookies

Need a break from the hustle and bustle of the holidays?
Snuggle up by the fireplace with a cold glass of milk and a
plate of these Ultimate Chocolate Comfort Cookies.
Because the recipe yields four dozen cookies, you'll have
plenty to share!

Project Instructions

Christmas decorating has never been easier! Our easy-to-follow instructions guide you, step-by-step, as you craft handmade projects that will fill your home with customized appeal. Refer to the General Instructions on page 185 for extra "how-to" tips and techniques.

Classic Cocoa & Cream

TABLE DRAPE
(shown on pages 8 – 9)

You will need brown and beige striped fabric, $\frac{1}{2}$"w paper-backed fusible web tape, tan beaded ball fringe, $1\frac{1}{2}$"w brown velvet ribbon, and $\frac{5}{8}$"w beige satin ribbon.

1. Cut fabric desired size plus $\frac{1}{2}$" for seam allowance on each edge.
2. Use web tape to hem raw edges of table drape.
3. Sew ball fringe just above each end of table drape. Turning ends under, sew a length of velvet ribbon over flange of fringe. Turning ends under, sew a length of satin ribbon just above velvet ribbon.

BRONZE URN CENTERPIECE
(shown on page 10)

You will need floral foam, 8"-tall ceramic bronze-footed urn, craft glue, greening pins, natural reindeer moss, wire cutters, pliers, magnolia swag or spray, foxtail greenery garland, large cedar pick, pussy willow stems, tallow berry stems, floral picks, and green floral tape.

1. Shape foam to fit in urn. Layer and glue foam in urn. Use greening pins to cover foam with moss.
2. Referring to *Assembling Arrangements*, page 185, and photo and taping short-stemmed items to floral picks, clip and arrange swag, foxtail garland, cedar pick, pussy willow stems, and berry stems in urn.

TABLESCAPE
(shown on pages 8 – 10)

You will need green floral tape, floral picks, wire cutters, pliers, magnolia swag or spray, foxtail greenery garland, large cedar pick, tallow berry stems, micro-beaded pears, clear and silver matte ball ornaments, and a hot glue gun.

Referring to *Assembling Arrangements*, page 185, and photo and taping short-stemmed items to floral picks, clip and arrange swag, foxtail garland, cedar pick, and berry stems around base of Bronze Urn Centerpiece. Hot glue pears and ornaments to tablescape as desired.

PEAR PLACE CARD HOLDERS
(shown on page 8)

You will need tracing paper, transfer paper, cream cardstock, white vellum paper, gold paint pen, brown gel pen, vellum tape, needle, wire cutters, crystal beaded-leaf garland, micro-beaded pears, and needle-nose pliers.

1. For each place card holder, trace, then transfer large star pattern, page 168, onto cardstock. Trace small star pattern, page 168, onto vellum; outline star and add name with gold pen. Outline name with brown pen. Cut out stars.
2. Tape stars together; use needle to pierce a hole through top of stars.
3. Cut a length of beaded-leaf garland. Separate wires; wrap one wire around pear stem. Attach star to remaining wire; using pliers, curl wire end to secure.

DINNER NAPKINS
(shown on page 8)

You will need taupe linen, $1/4$"w olive velvet ribbon, fabric glue, $1^3/8$"w tan wire-edged ribbon, white vellum, gold paint pen, needle, wire cutters, crystal beaded-leaf garland, and needle-nose pliers.

1. Cut an $18^1/2$" square from linen for each napkin. Press edges $1/4$" to wrong side twice; topstitch.

2. Cut four 18" velvet ribbon lengths. Covering topstitch seams, glue ribbon to front of napkin; trim ribbon ends.
3. Tie wire-edged ribbon around folded napkin; trim ribbon ends.
4. Trace large star pattern, page 168, onto vellum; cut out and outline star with gold pen. Use needle to pierce a hole through top of star.
5. Cut a length of beaded-leaf garland. Separate wires; wrap one wire around ribbon knot. Attach star to remaining wire; using pliers, curl wire end to secure.

MONOGRAMMED CHAIR BACK COVERS
(shown on pages 8 – 9)

You will need a computer printout of desired monogram enlarged to desired size (we enlarged the "R" from Textile font to 5" x $6^3/4$"), paper-backed fusible web, brown fabric for monogram, tan fabric for covers, $1/4$"w and $1^1/2$"w brown velvet ribbon, tan beaded ball fringe, and fabric glue.

Use a $1/2$" seam allowance for all sewing.

1. For each cover, print sized monogram in reverse. Trace the reversed letter on paper side of fusible web. Fuse web pattern to wrong side of brown fabric; cut out along drawn lines and remove paper backing.

2. Measure from chair seat, over chair back, then back to chair seat; add 2". Measure width of chair back and add 2". Cut out each cover using determined measurements.
3. Press each edge $1/2$" to wrong side twice; topstitch.
4. Fuse monogram to cover, 7" from one short edge. Using a medium-width zigzag stitch, machine satin stitch around raw edges of monogram.
5. Covering topstitch seams, glue $1/4$"w ribbon along side edges of cover; trim ribbon ends. Glue ball fringe across monogrammed end of cover. Turning ends to wrong sides, glue $1^1/2$"w ribbon over flange of fringe.
6. For ties, cut four $12^1/4$" lengths from $1^1/2$"w ribbon. Place cover on chair. Pin ties at desired height on each side of chair; sew in place. Glue a ball from fringe to end of each tie.

CHANDELIER LAMP SHADES
(shown on pages 8 – 9)

You will need brown and tan gingham fabric, self-adhesive lamp shade kits, fabric glue, tan beaded ball fringe, and $1/4$"w brown velvet ribbon.

1. Follow manufacturer's instructions to cover each lamp shade with fabric.

2. Glue flange of fringe along inside bottom rim of covered shade.
3. Glue a ribbon length around shade $1/4$" from top and bottom rims.

MAGNOLIA LEAF WREATH

(shown on page 11)

You will need pussy willow stems, floral wire, wire cutters, 30" dia. magnolia leaf wreath, magnolia bud picks, magnolia blossoms, hot glue gun, cedar picks, foxtail greenery garland, tallow berry stems, and crystal beaded-leaf garland.

1. Refer to photo to wire pussy willow stems to wreath. Wire magnolia bud picks, then blossoms to wreath.
2. Clipping as needed, hot glue cedar picks, foxtail garland, berry stems, and beaded-leaf garland to wreath for filler.

SPARKLING PUNCH

If you prefer a punch that is less sweet, just add additional sparkling water to taste.

1   can (11.5 ounces) frozen pineapple-orange juice concentrate, thawed and undiluted

1   can (6 ounces) frozen lemonade concentrate, thawed and undiluted
1   can (12 ounces) or 1 ¹/₂ cups ginger ale, chilled
1   bottle (750 milliliters) sparkling white grape juice, chilled
2   cups bottled sparkling water, chilled

Stir together concentrates in punch bowl. Add remaining ingredients, stirring gently. Serve immediately.
Yield: about 2 quarts

SPICY CASHEWS

¹/₄   cup butter or margarine
¹/₄   cup vegetable oil
2   jars (7 ounces each) dry-roasted cashews
¹/₂   teaspoon salt
¹/₄   to ¹/₂ teaspoon ground red pepper
¹/₂   teaspoon chili powder

Melt butter with oil in a large skillet over medium heat; add cashews, and cook 3 to 5 minutes or until browned. Remove cashews, and drain on paper towels; place in a bowl.
Combine salt, ground red pepper, and chili powder in a small bowl. Sprinkle over warm cashews, tossing to coat.
Yield: 3 cups cashews

FOCACCIA WITH ROSEMARY

Use focaccia for sandwiches or serve it when you want to add an authentic Italian touch to any meal. Cube and toast leftovers to make flavorful croutons.

2   envelopes (¹/₄ ounce each) active dry yeast
2   cups warm water (105° to 115°)
6   cups all-purpose flour, divided
¹/₂   cup unsalted butter, softened
¹/₂   cup finely chopped fresh rosemary leaves, divided
1   teaspoon salt
¹/₂   cup olive oil, divided
8   cloves garlic, minced
2   teaspoons kosher salt
¹/₂   teaspoon freshly ground pepper

Combine yeast and warm water in a 2-cup liquid glass measuring cup, and let stand 5 minutes.
Place 4 cups flour in a large bowl; make a well in center. Add yeast mixture; stir until a soft dough forms.
Cover dough, and let rise in a warm place (85°), free from drafts, 1 hour or until doubled in bulk.
Sprinkle remaining 2 cups flour on a flat surface. Turn dough out onto floured surface, and knead until flour is incorporated to make a firm dough. Gradually knead in butter, ¹/₄ cup rosemary, and salt.
Knead until dough is smooth and elastic (about 5 minutes), adding additional flour, if necessary.

Brush two 15 x 10 x 1-inch jellyroll pans with 2 tablespoons olive oil. Set aside.

Divide dough in half. Roll each portion into a 15 x 10-inch rectangle. Place in prepared pans. Using fingertips, press small indentations in top of dough; sprinkle with garlic and remaining 1/4 cup rosemary. Drizzle with remaining 6 tablespoons olive oil, and sprinkle with kosher salt and pepper.

Cover dough, and let rise in a warm place (85°), free from drafts, 30 to 45 minutes or until almost doubled in bulk.

Bake at 375° for 25 to 30 minutes or until golden. Cut into squares.
Yield: 2 loaves

Smoked Salmon with Capers

- 3/4 **pound sliced smoked salmon**
- 2 **tablespoons capers**
- 2 **green onions, minced**
- 2 **tablespoons caper juice or lemon juice**
- 1 **teaspoon sugar**
- 1 **carton (8 ounces) sour cream**
- 1 **pound thin-sliced black bread**

Arrange smoked salmon on a platter. Mix capers, green onion, caper juice, and sugar. Spoon over salmon. Serve with sour cream and black bread.
Yield: 16 appetizer servings

Herb-Marinated Olives

- 1/2 **cup olive oil**
- 1/3 **cup sherry vinegar or other flavored vinegar**
- 1 **tablespoon chopped fresh thyme or 1 teaspoon dried thyme**
- 1 **teaspoon fresh or 1/4 teaspoon dried rosemary**
- 1 1/2 **teaspoons chopped fresh oregano or 1/2 teaspoon dried oregano**
- 2 **cloves garlic, cut into slivers**
- 1 **dried red pepper pod (see Note)**
- 1 **jar (8 ounces) kalamata olives, drained, or 1 can (7.25 ounces) colossal ripe, pitted olives, drained**
- 1 **jar (7 ounces) green pimiento-stuffed olives, drained**
  Garnish: fresh herb sprigs

Combine first 7 ingredients in a bowl; stir well. Place olives in a large heavy-duty, zip-top plastic bag. Pour marinade over olives. Seal bag securely. Marinate in refrigerator 8 hours or up to 5 days, turning occasionally. Garnish, if desired.
Yield: 22 appetizer servings
Note: Find red pepper pods with other spices and herbs in specialty markets.

Pear Citrus Salad

For a complete meal, top with grilled chicken strips or canned albacore tuna.

- 3 **tablespoons cider vinegar**
- 2 **tablespoons vegetable oil**
- 1 **tablespoon sugar**
- 1/4 **teaspoon salt**
- 8 **cups torn salad greens**
- 2 **oranges, peeled and sectioned**
- 1 **large grapefruit, peeled and sectioned**
- 2 **pears, peeled and thinly sliced**
- 2 **tablespoons chopped walnuts, toasted (optional)**

Whisk together first 4 ingredients. Place greens in a large bowl. Add orange sections and next 2 ingredients. Drizzle with dressing, tossing gently to coat. Sprinkle with walnuts, if desired. Serve immediately.
Yield: 6 servings

ROASTED CHICKEN AND MUSHROOM SOUP

This is a thick soup, with a wonderfully hearty and nutty taste.

- 1 box (6 ounces) long-grain and wild rice mix
- 1 tablespoon olive oil
- 1¹/₂ cups chopped red onion
- 1 cup chopped celery
- 1 cup chopped carrot
- 2 garlic cloves, chopped
- 1 package (8 ounces) mushrooms, halved
- ¹/₄ cup all-purpose flour
- ¹/₂ teaspoon dried tarragon
- ¹/₄ teaspoon dried thyme
- 2¹/₄ cups water
- 2 tablespoons dry sherry
- 2 cans (14 ounces each) chicken broth
- 1 can (12 ounces) evaporated milk
- 3 cups shredded, roasted skinless chicken

Prepare rice according to package directions; set aside. Heat oil in a large Dutch oven over medium-high heat. Add chopped onion and next 4 ingredients (onion through mushrooms), and sauté for 6 minutes or until onion is tender. Lightly spoon flour into a dry measuring cup, and level with a knife. Stir flour, tarragon, and thyme into onion mixture, and cook for 1 minute, stirring frequently. Add 2¹/₄ cups water, sherry, broth, and evaporated milk; bring mixture to a boil. Reduce heat, and simmer for 20 minutes or until slightly thick. Stir in cooked rice and chicken; cook for 10 minutes or until thoroughly heated.
Yield: 8 servings (1¹/₂ cups each)

ZESTY HOLLANDAISE SAUCE

(shown on page 10)

This is a perfect sauce for asparagus.

- 3 egg yolks
- ¹/₈ teaspoon salt
- ¹/₄ teaspoon ground red pepper or to taste
- 2 tablespoons lemon juice
- ¹/₂ cup butter or margarine, cut into pieces

Whisk first 3 ingredients in top of a double boiler; gradually add lemon juice, stirring constantly. Add about one-third of butter to egg mixture; cook over hot, not boiling, water, stirring constantly with a wire whisk until butter melts. Add another third of butter, stirring constantly. As sauce thickens, stir in remaining butter. Cook until temperature reaches 160°, stirring constantly.

Remove sauce from double boiler; serve immediately.
Yield: ³/₄ cup sauce

ROSEMARY PORK TENDERLOIN

(shown on page 10)

- 1 tablespoon olive oil
- 1 pork tenderloin (1 pound), trimmed and cut crosswise into 12 (1-inch) slices
- ¹/₂ teaspoon salt
- ¹/₂ teaspoon freshly ground black pepper
- ¹/₂ cup dry white wine
- 1 tablespoon chopped fresh or 1 teaspoon dried rosemary
- 2 tablespoons water
- 1 teaspoon cornstarch
- ¹/₂ cup cranberry chutney

Heat the oil in a large nonstick skillet over medium-high heat. Sprinkle pork with salt and pepper. Add pork to pan; sauté for 5 minutes, turning once.

Add wine and rosemary to pan; bring to a boil. Cover, reduce heat, and simmer for 6 minutes. Combine water and cornstarch in a small bowl. Remove pork from pan; keep warm. Add cornstarch mixture to pan; bring to a boil. Cook 1 minute or until thick, stirring constantly. Serve the pork with sauce and chutney.
Yield: 4 servings

SCALLOPED POTATOES

(shown on page 10)

1 shallot, minced
1 large clove garlic, minced
$\frac{1}{2}$ teaspoon dried crushed red pepper
3 tablespoons butter or margarine, melted
$1\frac{1}{2}$ cups whipping cream
$1\frac{1}{4}$ cups milk
$\frac{1}{2}$ teaspoon salt
$\frac{1}{4}$ teaspoon freshly ground pepper
$2\frac{1}{2}$ pounds red potatoes, unpeeled and cut into $\frac{1}{8}$" slices
1 cup (4 ounces) shredded Gruyère cheese
$\frac{1}{4}$ cup freshly grated Parmesan cheese

Cook first 3 ingredients in butter in a Dutch oven over medium heat, stirring constantly, until tender. Add whipping cream and next 3 ingredients; bring to a boil, stirring occasionally. Stir in potato.

Spoon mixture into a lightly greased $2\frac{1}{2}$-quart shallow baking dish; sprinkle with cheeses.

Bake at 350° for 1 hour or until potato is tender. (Cover with aluminum foil the last 10 minutes of baking, if necessary, to prevent excessive browning.) Let stand, covered, 10 minutes.
Yield: 8 servings

EASY PERFECT CHOCOLATE CAKE

(shown on page 11)

1 package (18.25 ounces) devil's food cake mix with pudding
3 large eggs
$1\frac{1}{4}$ cups water
$\frac{1}{2}$ cup vegetable oil
Whipped Cream Filling
Creamy Chocolate Frosting
Garnishes: raspberries, chocolate curls (see Note) and powdered sugar

Beat first 4 ingredients at medium speed with an electric mixer 2 minutes. Pour batter into 2 greased and floured 9-inch round cakepans.

Bake at 350° for 25 minutes or until a wooden pick inserted in center comes out clean. Cool in pans on wire racks 10 minutes; remove from pans, and cool completely on wire racks. Cover and chill 1 hour.

Spread Whipped Cream Filling between layers. Spread Creamy Chocolate Frosting on top and sides of cake. Garnish with raspberries, chocolate curls, and powdered sugar. Store in refrigerator.
Yield: one 2-layer cake
Note: For chocolate curls, melt about 5 chocolate squares and pour into a jellyroll pan; spread chocolate over pan. Chill about 10 minutes. Scrape across surface of chocolate with a long metal spatula or knife. Return pan to refrigerator if chocolate becomes too soft. Use a toothpick to pick up curls.

WHIPPED CREAM FILLING

1 cup whipping cream
$\frac{1}{4}$ cup powdered sugar
1 teaspoon vanilla extract

Beat all ingredients at medium speed with an electric mixer until stiff peaks form.
Yield: about 2 cups filling

CREAMY CHOCOLATE FROSTING

1 cup (6 ounces) semisweet chocolate morsels
$\frac{1}{2}$ cup half-and-half
1 cup butter or margarine
$2\frac{1}{2}$ cups powdered sugar

Cook first 3 ingredients in a heavy saucepan over medium heat, stirring until chocolate melts. Remove from heat; cool 15 minutes. Stir in powdered sugar.

Place pan in a bowl filled with ice, and beat at medium speed with an electric mixer about 8 minutes or until frosting reaches spreading consistency.
Yield: 3 cups frosting

Olde World Radiance

For this section we purchased two fringed jacquard throws. One throw was used for the Embellished Throw and the other was used for accents and remaining projects in the section...the Mantel Scarf, Boxed Pillow, Tufted Throw Pillow, and the Cone-Shaped Stocking.

MADONNA AND CHILD PAINTING
(shown on page 15)

You will need assorted acrylic paints (we used burnt umber, golden brown, light ivory, and cherry red), paintbrushes, 24" x 30" stretched canvas (gallery-wrap style), transfer paper, matte medium, hot glue gun, flat trim, and decorative tacks.

Refer to Painting Techniques, pages 185 – 186, before beginning project.

1. Basecoat canvas ivory. Enlarge pattern, page 169, 287%. Transfer image to canvas.

2. Using matte medium to help blend colors, refer to photo to paint canvas.
3. Hot glue trim along edges of canvas. Spacing evenly, insert tacks along center of trim.

LUSTROUS CANDLESTICKS AND EMBELLISHED CANDLES
(shown on page 13)

You will need a hot glue gun, beaded trim, candlesticks, flat trim, tracing paper, removable tape, pillar candles, gold sequin pins, and 2mm and 4mm round amber beads.

Never leave a burning candle unattended.

1. For each candlestick, hot glue a length of beaded trim around candlestick. Glue flat trim over flange of beaded trim.
2. For candles, trace background and fleur-de-lis patterns, page 168, onto tracing paper. Tape pattern to candle, then use a straight pin to make holes along pattern lines to mark pattern on candle; remove pattern.
3. Referring to photos, starting in the middle, and working outward, insert pins through beads into candle, forming design.

TABLE SCARF
(shown on page 15)

You will need a 22½" x 66" strip of fabric (we cut our strip from a fringed jacquard throw; the strip was cut the length of the throw with the fringe along the ends), fabric glue, beaded trim, and flat trim.

1. Matching right sides, sew long edges of fabric strip together. Turn scarf right side out; press.
2. Turning ends under, glue a length of beaded trim just above fringe on scarf; allow to dry. Turning ends under, glue flat trim over flange of beaded trim; allow to dry.

MOSSY PINECONE ORNAMENTS
(shown on page 14)

For each ornament, you will need craft glue, medium green acrylic paint, paintbrush, pinecone, clear microbeads, 9" length of ½"w green silk ribbon, 10mm gold bead, and a hot glue gun.

1. Thoroughly mix one part glue with one part paint. Brush mixture onto pinecone.

2. While mixture is still wet, sprinkle microbeads over pinecone; allow to dry. Once dry, shake off excess beads.

3. For hanger, fold ribbon length in half, then thread ribbon ends through bead. Knot ribbon ends below bead, then trim excess. Hot glue knot to top of ornament.

BOXED PILLOW
(shown on page 14)

You will need fusible interfacing; 11" fabric square; flat trim; two 7" squares of paper-backed fusible web; 7" square of gold velvet; 7" square of green satin; 5mm bugle and 2mm and 4mm round gold beads; four 1½" dia. buttons from a covered button kit; fabric to cover buttons (we used the reverse side of the same fabric we used for the square); 17" square box pillow; upholstery needle; heavy-duty thread; four 1" dia. buttons for back of pillow.

1. Fuse interfacing to wrong side of 11" fabric square. Sew trim along outer edges of fabric square.

2. Enlarge background and fleur-de-lis patterns, page 168, 138%.

3. Follow *Making Appliqués*, page 186, and use enlarged patterns to make background appliqué from velvet and fleur-de-lis appliqué from satin.

4. Fuse fleur-de-lis to background, then fuse background to center of fabric square.

5. Referring to photo, sew bugle beads along outer edges of background piece and sew 2mm beads along edges of fleur-de-lis pieces. Sew 4mm beads inside fleur-de-lis circles.

6. Follow manufacturer's instructions to cover the 1½" dia. buttons with fabric.

7. Position fabric square on pillow. To sew a covered button at each corner of fabric square and tuft pillow, begin on back side of pillow and use the upholstery needle and heavy-duty thread to sew through a 1" button, up through the pillow, through the covered button, then back down through the pillow and the 1" button. Pull the threads and tightly knot together to secure.

TUFTED THROW PILLOW
(shown on page 14)

You will need fabric glue, beaded trim, 16" dia. tufted pillow, flat trim, one 2½" dia. button from a covered button kit, and a scrap of coordinating fabric to cover button.

1. Glue beaded trim along outer top edge of pillow; allow to dry. Folding ends under, glue flat trim over flange of beaded trim; allow to dry.

2. Follow manufacturer's instructions to cover button with fabric. Tack covered button to pillow over existing button on pillow.

EMBELLISHED THROW
(shown on page 14)

You will need ten 9" squares of paper-backed fusible web, five 9" squares of gold velvet, five 9" squares of green satin, 51" x 66" fringed jacquard throw, 5mm gold bugle beads, 2mm round gold beads, beaded trim, and flat trim.

1. For each fleur-de-lis (we made five), follow Steps 2 – 3 of Boxed Pillow, this page, enlarging patterns 188%. Fuse fleur-de-lis to backgrounds. Remove paper backing from backgrounds, then spacing evenly, fuse them along one fringed edge of throw.

2. Follow Step 5 of Boxed Pillow, to bead the fleurs-de-lis (using 2mm beads around the circles instead of the 4mm beads).

3. Turning ends under, sew a length of beaded trim just above fringe on throw. Turning ends under, sew a length of flat trim over flange of beaded trim.

BRONZE URN ARRANGEMENTS
(shown on page 15)

For each arrangement, you will need floral foam, 12"-tall bronze urn, craft glue, sand, floral picks, sheet moss, medium green acrylic paint, paintbrush, clear microbeads, twigs, artificial noble fir, artificial berry with greenery stems, and red beaded cascades.

1. Shape and layer pieces of foam to fit in urn; glue foam in urn, then allow to dry. Add sand to urn to fill holes and weight urn.
2. Use floral picks to cover foam with sheet moss.
3. Follow Steps 1 and 2 of Mossy Pinecone Ornaments, page 128, to add beads to twigs.
4. Referring to *Assembling Arrangements*, page 185, and photo, arrange greenery, berries, cascades, then twigs in urn until desired look is achieved.

FLEUR-DE-LIS ORNAMENTS
(shown on page 14)

For each ornament, you will need a double-sided adhesive sheet, red glass ball ornament, red metallic microbeads, découpage glue, gold embossing powder, and a soft bristle paintbrush.

1. Enlarge or reduce fleur-de-lis pattern, page 168, as needed to fit ornament. Trace onto adhesive sheet; cut out. Remove paper backing from one side and adhere to ornament. Remove remaining paper, then sprinkle microbeads over adhesive. Shake off excess beads.
2. Referring to photo, apply glue around design. While glue is still wet, sprinkle with embossing powder; shake off excess. Once dry, use brush to gently remove any excess powder from beaded area.

CONE-SHAPED STOCKING
(shown on page 15)

You will need fabric for stocking and lining, fringed fabric for cuff (we used part of a fringed jacquard throw), beaded trim, flat trim, one 1¼" dia. button from a covered button kit, and a 3½" long tassel with hanger.

Use a ½" seam allowance for all sewing unless otherwise indicated.

1. Enlarge cone pattern, page 168, 336%. Using pattern, cut two cone shapes from fabric.
2. For each cone, match right sides and sew long edges together; press. Turn one cone right side out.
3. Press top edges of each cone ½" to wrong side.

4. Matching wrong sides and seams, place one cone inside the other cone.
5. With fringe running the length of the strip, cut a 5" x 31" strip from fringed end of cuff fabric. Sew a length of beaded trim just above fringe. Sew flat trim over flange of beaded trim. Matching right sides, sew ends of strip together.
6. With wrong side facing outward and aligning seams, insert ½" of raw edge of cuff between top edges of cones; pin in place. Topstitching along edges of the cones, sew cuff in place. Turn cuff to right side of stocking.
7. For hanger, cut a 1¼" x 9½" strip from cuff fabric. Press one long edge ¼" to wrong side; overlapping pressed edge over raw edge, press long edges to center back. Sew down center of strip. Matching ends, tack holder to back of stocking. Follow manufacturer's instructions to cover button with cuff fabric, then sew button to base of hanger (Fig. 1).

Fig. 1

8. Pinch bottom of stocking to a point and tack in place. Trimming hanger to fit as desired, sew tassel hanger to point of stocking.

Retro Noel

PAINTED STAR ORNAMENTS
(shown on page 18)

For each ornament, you will need tracing paper, cardstock, acrylic paint (we used dark pink and medium green), paintbrushes, craft glue, mica flakes, $1/8$" dia. hole punch, and decorative fiber trim.

1. Using star pattern, page 171, cut star from cardstock.
2. Paint both sides and edges of star; allow to dry.
3. Apply glue to one side of star. While glue is still wet, sprinkle mica flakes onto star. Once dry, shake off excess flakes. Repeat for remaining side of star.
4. For hanger, punch a hole in top of star. Thread a length of fiber trim through hole and knot ends.

PAINTED GLASS BALLS
(shown on page 18)

You will need $2^{1}/_{2}$" and 3" dia. iridescent glass ornaments with metal end caps; assorted acrylic paints (we used light pink, dark pink, light brown, and cream); matte medium; small plastic cups; cotton swabs; craft glue; and mica flakes.

1. Remove end cap from each ornament. Mix desired paint color with matte medium until a thin consistency is achieved. Pour paint mixture into ornament.

2. Covering opening with a paper towel, swirl paint mixture around, coating inside of ornament.
3. To drain excess paint, place ornament upside down in a cup. Once excess paint has drained, place ornaments on their sides, facing a fan until dry.
4. Carefully replace end cap.
5. Using a cotton swab, apply glue around top of ornament as desired and on end cap. While glue is still wet, sprinkle mica flakes onto ornament. Once dry, shake off excess flakes.

MIRRORED STARS
(shown on page 19)

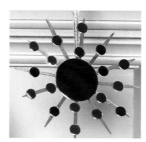

For each ornament, you will need silver spray paint, twelve craft picks cut to $2^{1}/_{2}$", household cement, two 2" dia. mirrors, thirty-six $1/2$" dia. mirrors, $1/8$"w ribbon, and decorative trim.

Use spray paint and household cement in a well-ventilated area. Allow paint and cement to dry after each application.

1. Paint both sides of craft picks.
2. Use cement to adhere evenly spaced craft picks to back of one 2" dia. mirror.
3. Adhere eighteen $1/2$" dia. mirrors along craft sticks.
4. For hanging loop, adhere ends of a length of ribbon and a length of trim to back of center mirror.
5. Adhere matching mirrors to back of ornament.

SERENITY VASE
(shown on page 19)

You will need a glass vase; rubbing alcohol; cotton balls; removable tape; assorted glass paints (we used light pink, dark pink, light brown, dark brown, yellow, and medium green); paintbrushes; clear gloss glaze glass sealer; mica flakes; medium-gauge floral wire; wire cutters; white floral tape; 6mm round pink faceted beads; hot glue gun; and frosted greenery picks.

Use alcohol in a well-ventilated area.

1. Use alcohol and cotton balls to clean outside of vase.
2. Enlarge or reduce pattern, page 170, to fit vase. Tape pattern inside vase.
3. Paint design basecoats; allow to dry. Paint details on designs; allow to dry. Apply sealer; allow to dry.
4. Remove pattern, then fill vase with mica flakes.
5. For pink picks, join two 18" lengths of wire by wrapping floral tape around bottom $4^{1}/_{2}$" of wires. Adding a dot of glue to first bead to keep beads from slipping off, thread beads onto wires. Use pliers to bend top ends of wires into loops, trimming excess wire if necessary. Glue three beads in a triangle to wire loop.
6. Arrange greenery and pink picks in vase as desired.

GLASS CANDLEHOLDERS
(shown on page 18)

You will need clear glass candleholders, rubbing alcohol, cotton balls, removable tape, assorted glass paints (we used light pink, dark pink, light brown, dark brown, yellow, and medium green), paintbrushes, clear gloss glaze glass sealer, and candles to fit holders.

Never leave burning candles unattended. Use alcohol in a well-ventilated area.

1. Use alcohol and cotton balls to clean outside of vase.
2. For each candleholder, enlarge desired design from pattern, page 170, to fit candleholder.
3. Tape pattern inside candleholder.
4. Paint design basecoats; allow to dry. Paint details on design; allow to dry. Apply sealer; allow to dry.
5. Remove pattern, then place candles in holders.

RETRO PAPIER-MÂCHÉ ORNAMENTS
(shown on page 18)

For each ornament, you will need white spray primer, assorted colors of acrylic paint, paintbrushes, papier-mâché shape (we used 4" dia. ovals, 3" x 4" rectangles, and 3³⁄₄" dia. circles), clear acrylic spray sealer, tracing paper, transfer paper, stylus, silver paint pen, craft glue, and mica flakes.

Oval Ornament

Use spray primer and sealer in a well-ventilated area.

1. Prime, then paint basecoats on background and on sides of ornament.
2. Transfer design, page 172, onto shape.
3. Referring to photo, paint design. If desired, use paint pen to accent design. Apply sealer.
4. Apply glue along sides of ornament. While glue is still wet, sprinkle mica flakes onto ornament. Once dry, shake off excess flakes.

Rectangle Ornament

Follow Oval Ornament instructions, using rectangle pattern, page 171, and referring to photo to paint ornament.

Circle Ornament

Follow Oval Ornament instructions, using circle pattern, page 171, and referring to photo to paint ornament.

SQUARE TREE SKIRT
(shown on page 18)

You will need a rotary cutter and cutting mat; ³⁄₄ yd of light brown fabric; and ¹⁄₈ yd each of dark brown, yellow, green, dark pink, cream, and light pink fabric; fabric glue; and 4mm round clear beads.

Use the rotary cutter and cutting mat for all cutting.

1. For skirt, cut a 26" square from light brown fabric. Press edges ¹⁄₂" to wrong side twice; topstitch.
2. Cut thirty-five 1¹⁄₂" squares each from dark brown and yellow fabric, forty-five 1¹⁄₂" squares each from green and dark pink fabric, and forty-eight 1¹⁄₂" squares each from cream and light pink fabric.
3. Arrange squares on skirt. Apply a small dot of glue to center of wrong side of each square, then adhere squares to skirt; allow to dry.
4. Sew one bead to center of each square.
5. Refer to Fig. 1 to cut skirt to wrap around tree.

Fig. 1

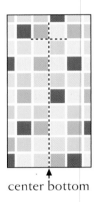

center bottom

VELLUM ORNAMENTS
(shown on page 18)

For each ornament, you will need a 1⁵⁄₈" square punch, clear acetate sheets, patterned vellum, ³⁄₄" dia. circle punch, ¹⁄₈" dia. hole punch, silver jump rings, and ¹⁄₈"w ribbon.

1. Punch two squares from acetate and one from vellum.
2. Punch one ³⁄₄" dia. circle from vellum.

3. Layer vellum square between acetate squares, then use hole punch to punch a hole through top and bottom of squares. Attach a jump ring through each set of holes.
4. Punch a hole in vellum circle; attach a jump ring through hole.
5. Use jump rings to attach circle to squares.
6. For hanger, thread a length of ribbon through top jump ring and knot ends.

RIBBON GARLAND
(shown on page 18)

You will need craft glue, patterned and white vellum, white paper, craft knife and cutting mat, $^{1}/_{8}$"w ribbon, and stickers.

We made two 60" lengths of garland for our tabletop tree.

1. For circles, layer and glue patterned vellum on white paper; allow to dry, then cut out circles. For squares, cut approximately $1^{1}/_{4}$" square shapes from white vellum.
2. Cut slit(s) in shapes and thread ribbon through, OR adhere a sticker or sticker backing to shape and thread ribbon through a cut out area, OR simply place ribbon between shape and sticker. Knot ribbon ends to secure shapes.

RETRO STOCKINGS
(shown on page 19)

For each stocking, you will need two 12" x 20" pieces of light pink fabric for stocking; paper-backed fusible web; dark pink fabric for toe and heel; two 12" x 20" pieces of white fabric for lining; 9$^{1}/_{2}$" x 14" piece of tan fabric for cuff; light pink, dark pink, dark brown, yellow, and green fabric for squares (we cut 52 squares); rotary cutter and cutting mat; fabric glue; 4mm round clear beads; and an 8$^{1}/_{2}$" length of $^{7}/_{8}$"w ribbon.

Use a $^{1}/_{2}$" seam allowance for all sewing.

1. Enlarge stocking pattern, page 171, 172%; cut out. Use pattern to cut out stocking front and back (one in reverse).
2. Follow *Making Appliqués*, page 186, to make two heel and two toe appliqués (one each in reverse) from dark pink fabric.
3. Fuse, then using a decorative stitch, machine sew toe and heel pieces along inner edges to stocking front and back.
4. Matching right sides and leaving top edges open, sew stocking pieces together. Clip curves, then turn right side out.
5. Use stocking pattern to cut out front and back lining pieces (one in reverse). Matching right sides and leaving top edges open, sew lining pieces together. Clip curves; do not turn right side out. With wrong sides together and matching seams, insert lining into stocking. Baste lining to stocking along top edges.
6. Matching right sides, sew ends of cuff together to form a ring; press seam open. Turn right side out. Matching wrong sides and raw edges, fold cuff in half. Matching raw edges and seam in cuff to heel side seam of stocking, insert cuff into top of stocking; sew cuff to stocking along raw edges. Turn cuff to outside.
7. For each color square, fuse two pieces of the same color fabric together. Use rotary cutter and cutting mat to cut 1" squares from each fabric color. Position squares on cuff. Apply a small dot of glue to center on wrong side of each square and adhere to cuff.

8. Sew one bead to center of each square, being sure to only sew through cuff.
9. For hanger, fold ribbon in half and tack inside stocking at heel side seam.

VELLUM MOBILE
(shown on page 18)

You will need a 1$^{5}/_{8}$" square punch; 3" dia. circle punch; clear acetate sheets; patterned vellum; $^{1}/_{8}$" dia. hole punch; silver jump rings; 8", 7$^{1}/_{2}$", 7", and 5$^{1}/_{2}$" lengths of medium-gauge wire; needle-nose pliers; lightweight string; and small plastic snowflakes.

1. For each circle and square, punch two shapes each from acetate and one each from vellum.
2. Layer vellum shapes between acetate shapes. Use hole punch to punch a hole through tops of squares and circles; punch additional holes in bottoms of several circles for connecting shapes. Attach jump rings through holes.
3. Use additional jump rings to connect shapes.
4. Use pliers to make loops in ends of wire lengths.
5. For hanger, tie one end of a length of string to a jump ring; tie remaining end of string to 8" wire.
6. Use string to attach shapes and snowflakes to wire.
7. Use another length of string to attach 7$^{1}/_{2}$" wire to 8" wire.
8. Repeat Steps 6 and 7 for remaining wire lengths, shapes, and snowflakes, making sure mobile is balanced as you go.

Merry & Bright

PAPIER-MÂCHÉ ORNAMENTS

(shown on page 26)

For each ornament, you will need white spray primer, assorted colors of acrylic paint, paintbrushes, papier-mâché shape (we used 3³/₄"w stars, 2" dia. turnip shapes, and 3"w x 4"h rectangles), clear acrylic spray sealer, hot glue gun, buttons, ¹/₁₆"w ribbon, 8mm painted wooden bead, ball-head straight pins, and transfer paper.

Use caution when working with glue gun. Use primer and sealer in a well-ventilated area. Allow primer, paint, and sealer to dry after each application.

Star

1. Prime, then paint star sections with alternating basecoats. Use end of paintbrush handle to paint dots. Apply sealer. Stack and glue buttons to center of star.
2. For hanger, knot ends of a length of ribbon, forming a loop. Hot glue knot inside bead. Hot glue hanger to ornament.

Turnip

1. Prime, then paint swirls on turnip shape. Dip pinheads into paint; allow to dry. Insert pins into shape along outer edge. Apply sealer.
2. For hanger, knot ends of a length of ribbon, forming a loop. Hot glue knot inside bead. If desired, hot glue bead onto buttons, then hot glue hanger to ornament.

Tree

1. Prime rectangle shape.
2. Transfer tree design, page 173, onto shape. Referring to photo, paint design, outlining diamonds and frames with white paint. Use end of paintbrush handle to paint dots. Apply sealer.
3. For hanger, knot ends of a length of ribbon, forming a loop. Hot glue knot inside bead. If desired, hot glue bead onto buttons, then hot glue hanger to ornament.

BUMP CHENILLE STARS

(shown on page 26)

For each star, you will need three bump chenille stems, hot glue gun, string, buttons, and six 8mm painted wooden beads.

1. Fold and hot glue each end of each stem to its center.
2. Layer stems, forming a star shape. Hot glue stems together at intersection; wrap and tie string around stems for added security.
3. Hot glue buttons to each side of star center. Thread beads onto ends of star points.
4. To hang, nestle star in branches of tree.

WOODEN TOP ORNAMENTS

(shown on page 26)

For each ornament, you will need one 8mm bead, one wooden yo-yo kit with center peg removed, one 1"h wooden candle cup, two 1¹/₂" dia. wooden rings, one 1¹/₄" miniature wooden Christmas tree, one 3" dia. wooden disk (if desired), wood glue, white spray primer, assorted colors of acrylic paint, paintbrushes, and clear acrylic spray sealer.

Use primer and sealer in a well-ventilated area. Allow glue, primer, paint, and sealer to dry after each application.

1. For hanger, thread bead onto a 9" length of yo-yo string. Thread ends of string through hole in candle cup, catching bead on inside; tie string ends into a knot.
2. Refer to Assembly Diagram to glue pieces together.
3. Prime, then paint ornament. Use end of paintbrush handle to paint dots. Apply sealer.

Assembly Diagram

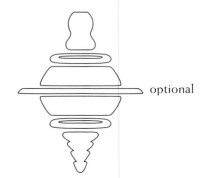

optional

Use primer and sealer in a well-ventilated area. When stacking your wooden pieces, be sure they are stable enough to hold a candle. Allow glue to dry after each application.

1. Glue wooden shapes and cutouts together to form candlesticks, as shown above.
2. Prime, then paint candlesticks. Use end of paintbrush handle to paint dots. Apply sealer.

PAINTED WOODEN CANDLESTICKS

(shown on page 22)

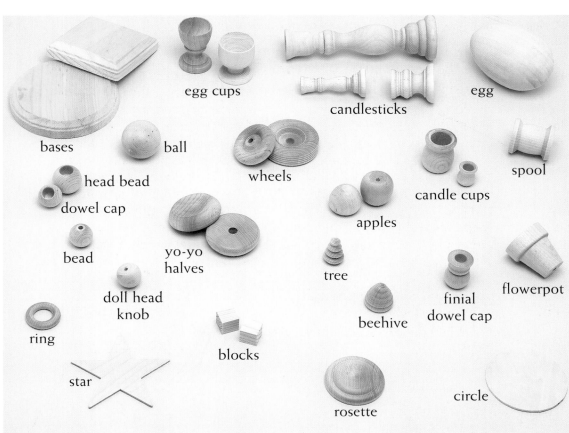

egg cups

candlesticks

egg

bases

ball

head bead

wheels

spool

dowel cap

candle cups

bead

apples

yo-yo halves

tree

doll head knob

finial dowel cap

flowerpot

ring

beehive

blocks

star

rosette

circle

For each candlestick, you will need wood glue, assorted wooden shapes and cutouts (we used the pieces shown on the left), white spray primer, assorted colors of acrylic paint, paintbrushes, and clear acrylic spray sealer.

FELT TABLE RUNNER
(shown on page 22)

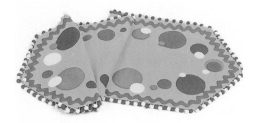

You will need assorted colors of felt, craft glue, two colors of pom-pom fringe, and jumbo rickrack.

Allow glue to dry after each application.

1. Cut a 17" x 48" strip from felt. Cut each end in a point.
2. With pom-pom colors alternating, layer and glue fringe along bottom edge of runner.
3. Glue rickrack along top edge of runner.
4. Cut assorted size circles from felt. Glue circles to runner.

TIP: To match ends of runner, fold felt in half and cut both points at the same time.

PAINTED WALL HANGING
(shown on page 25)

You will need unfinished canvas, gesso, yardstick, assorted colors of acrylic paint, paintbrushes, mat board, hot glue gun, chenille stems, wooden pegs, 1" wooden star cutout, dimensional foam dots, two $1/2$" dia. grommets and a grommet setter, 20"-long x $3/4$"w flat piece of wood, and 1"w grosgrain ribbon.

Refer to photo to cut canvas and paint wall hanging. Allow gesso and paint to dry after each application.

1. Cut a 21" x $31^1/2$" piece from canvas with wavy edges and pointed corners. To prime canvas, follow manufacturer's instructions to apply gesso to canvas.
2. Use yardstick to center and draw a 17" x 27" rectangle on primed side of canvas. Draw a 15" x 25" rectangle inside first rectangle.
3. Using yardstick, draw a line from corner to corner of inner rectangle, making an "X". Using the "X" as a guide, refer to Fig. 1 to draw diamonds and center rectangular shape.

Fig. 1

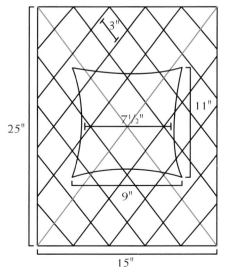

4. Paint basecoats on wall hanging. Use white paint to outline each section.
5. Cut a $7^1/2$" x $9^1/2$" piece from mat board. Draw around mat board on wrong side of another piece of canvas; cut out 1" outside drawn line. Wrapping to back, hot glue canvas to mat board.
6. Paint border and background on canvas-wrapped board. Use white paint to outline sections. Use end of paintbrush handle to paint dots.
7. Refer to Fig. 2 to form tree from chenille stems; hot glue in place on board.

Fig. 2

8. Paint pegs and star.
9. Use foam dots to attach board to wall hanging.
10. Hot glue pegs at diamond intersections and star to top of tree.
11. Follow manufacturer's instructions to attach grommets to top corners of wall hanging. Hot glue wood piece across back of wall hanging just above grommets.
12. Thread ends of ribbon through grommets and knot at front of wall hanging; notch ends of ribbon.

LUMINARIES
(shown on page 24)

You will need rubbing alcohol, cotton balls, small jars, assorted colors of glass paint, paintbrushes, and clear gloss glaze glass sealer.

Never leave a burning candle unattended. Use alcohol in a well-ventilated area. Several coats of paint may be necessary for desired coverage. Allow paint and sealer to dry after each application.

1. Use alcohol and cotton balls to clean outsides of jars.
2. Paint jars as desired. We used the shape of our glass jars as a guide to the paint stripes.
3. Use end of paintbrush handle to paint dots.
4. Apply sealer.

FELT ORNAMENTS
(shown on page 26)

You will need pinking shears, assorted colors of felt, craft glue, embroidery floss, cardboard, 12mm painted wooden bead, buttons, pom-pom fringe, and seed beads.

Use pinking shears for all cutting unless otherwise indicated. Allow glue to dry after each application.

Tree

1. For background, cut a 3¹/₂" tall tree shape from felt. Cut a tree from felt ¹/₄" smaller on all sides than background. Center and glue tree to background.

2. Cut, then glue a ¹/₄"w strip of felt along outer edge of tree.
3. Use regular scissors to cut, then glue felt circles to tree.
4. For tassel, follow *Making Tassels*, page 185, using floss and a 2" cardboard square. Thread bead and button onto tassel, then glue tassel to bottom of ornament.
5. For hanger, cut a ¹/₄" x 6" strip and a ¹/₂" x 6" strip from felt. Glue ¹/₄"w strip along center of ¹/₂"w strip. Matching ends, glue to back of ornament.

Package

1. For background, cut a 4" x 4¹/₂" piece from felt. Use regular scissors to cut a 3¹/₄" x 3¹/₂" piece from felt for package. Center and glue package to background.
2. Cut felt strips in varying widths from ³/₈"w to ³/₄"w. Weave, then glue strips to package.
3. Glue a length of pom-pom fringe along bottom of ornament. Glue a felt strip to flange of fringe. Glue seed beads along felt strip.
4. For hanger, follow Step 5 of Tree Ornament.

Swirl

1. For background, cut a 3⁵/₈" dia. circle from felt. Use regular scissors to cut a 3" dia. circle from felt. Center and glue circle to background.

2. For swirl, cut a ¹/₄" x 11" strip from felt. Shape and glue swirl to circle. Glue seed beads along swirl.
3. Cut three 3" strips from felt. Glue strips along outer edge of circle. Use regular scissors to cut, then glue small circles where strips meet.
4. For hanger, follow Step 5 of Tree Ornament.

ELF WREATH
(shown on page 27)

You will need nine chenille stems, hot glue gun, assorted wooden beads, floral picks, 18" salal wreath, T-pins, three Elves (page 138), medium-gauge craft wire, and wire cutters.

1. For each beaded garland section, twist and hot glue three chenille stems together at one end. Thread one large bead onto twisted end of chenille stems, then thread one smaller bead onto each chenille stem. Repeat threading one large bead, then three smaller beads until you reach the end of the stems. Twist and hot glue remaining ends together.
2. Use floral picks to secure garland sections to wreath.
3. Use T-pins to secure Elves to wreath.
4. For hanger, glue ends of a length of wire to back of wreath.

FELT STOCKINGS
(shown on page 24 – 25)

You will need assorted colors of felt, 1"w grosgrain ribbon, craft glue, assorted size pom-poms, pinking shears, and seed beads.

Allow glue to dry after each application. Use pinking shears as desired to cut felt pieces.

Stockings

1. Enlarge stocking and cuff patterns, pages 172 – 173, 111%. For each stocking, use patterns to cut two stocking shapes and one cuff from felt. Leaving top open, use a ¼" seam allowance and sew stocking shapes together. For hanger, tack ends of a length of ribbon inside stocking. With ends at back, glue top of cuff along top of stocking.
2. Glue pom-poms to points of cuff and stocking. Glue a ¼"w strip of felt along top edge of cuff; glue seed beads along strip.
3. Add Tree, Package, or Swirl Embellishments (below) to stocking. Cut, then glue felt circles to stocking; glue seed beads to centers of circles.

Embellishments

Trees

For trees stocking, cut a 2¾" tall background tree shape from felt. Cut a tree ¼" smaller on all sides than background. Center and glue tree to background. Cut, then glue a ¼"w strip of felt along outer edge of tree. Cut, then glue felt circles to tree. Glue trees to stocking. If necessary, trim trees along outer edge of stocking.

Packages

For packages stocking, cut 2¼" squares from felt. Cut felt strips in varying widths from ¼"w to ½"w. Weave, then glue strips to packages. Glue packages to stocking. If necessary, trim packages along outer edge of stocking.

Swirls

For swirls stocking, cut ¼" x 11" strips from felt. Shape and glue swirls to stocking. If necessary, trim swirls along outer edge of stocking. Glue seed beads along swirls.

ELVES
(shown on page 23)

You will need 18-gauge armature wire, wire cutters, wire pliers, green and red felt, freezer paper, pinking shears, fiberfill, craft glue, assorted size pom-poms, and wiggle eyes.

1. For body, refer to Fig. 1 to twist centers of two 12" lengths of wire together. Use pliers to form loops at each end of wires.

Fig. 1

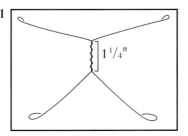

1¼"

2. Cut one 12" square each from red and green felt. Trace elf pattern, page 174, onto dull side of freezer paper. Iron shiny side of freezer paper onto green felt. With pattern on top, place wire body between green and red felt. Pin felt pieces together.
3. Referring to stitching lines on pattern, sew felt squares together, leaving points open. Use pinking shears to cut out elf ⅛" outside stitching line. Remove freezer paper. Using opening in head, stuff elf with fiberfill; sew openings closed.
4. For accessories, cut ten 6" squares from red felt. Trace one hat, two mittens, and two slippers, page 174, onto dull side of freezer paper. Iron shiny side of each freezer paper pattern onto one felt square. With a pattern piece on top, pin two felt squares together. Leaving openings for the hands, feet, and head, sew pieces together along pattern lines. Using regular scissors, cut out accessories just outside stitching line, then use pinking shears to trim openings of mittens, slippers, and brim of hat.
5. Glue pom-pom on point of hat, then glue accessories over head, hands, and feet.
6. Glue eyes, pom-pom nose, and mouth cut from felt to face and pom-pom buttons to body.

TREE TOPPER ELF
(shown on page 20)

For Tree Topper Elf, follow Elves, this page, twisting 2½" of centers of two 18" lengths of wire, enlarging patterns 174%, and using 17" pieces of felt for elf body and 7" squares of felt for accessories.

Winter Green

POM-POM GARLAND

(shown on page 29)

For quick tree garland, use fabric glue to adhere pom-poms to a length of ribbon. Wind the ribbon through your tree and you have instant pizzazz.

WRAPPED PACKAGES

(shown on page 30)

An easy, inexpensive way to decorate your mantel for the holidays is to wrap assorted-size boxes in different shades of green paper and fabric, then trim them with coordinating ribbons and pom-poms. Line the packages on the mantel and you're set.

FRAME PLACE CARD HOLDERS

(shown on page 33)

For each place card holder, you will need a 2$\frac{1}{2}$" x 3" wooden frame with backing, fabric, fabric glue, cardstock, and coordinating ribbons.

1. Draw around frame onto wrong side of fabric; cut out 2" outside drawn lines.
2. Remove backing from frame. Use fabric glue to adhere fabric to front of frame, pressing fabric into all grooves and around the edges of the frame.
3. Wrap and glue edges of fabric to back of frame.
4. Cut an "X" from corner to corner of fabric inside frame opening; wrap and glue fabric to back.
5. Cut a piece of cardstock to fit inside frame. Write name on cardstock, then secure cardstock in frame.
6. Glue a length of ribbon around frame. Glue a ribbon bow to top of place card holder.

GIFT BOX ORNAMENTS

(shown on page 31)

For each ornament, you will need 1$\frac{1}{2}$" x 2$\frac{1}{4}$" papier-mâché box with lid, green and lime green foil paper, double-sided tape, fabric glue, and $\frac{1}{4}$"w green ribbon.

1. Wrap box in green paper and lid in lime green paper, securing in place with tape as you go.
2. Gluing ends to bottom, wrap ribbon around box. Glue a ribbon bow to top of box.
3. For hanger, thread a length of ribbon under ribbon on one side of box. Overlapping slightly, glue ribbon ends together.

RIBBON CENTERPIECE

(shown on page 33)

You will need assorted shades and widths of green ribbon, assorted candles, medium-gauge craft wire, wire cutters, and assorted shades of green beads.

Never leave a burning candle unattended.

1. For candles, cut ribbon lengths long enough to tie around candles plus streamers.
2. Arrange candles on table. Knot a ribbon length around each candle; arrange streamers on table as desired.
3. For each beaded garland, twist ends of two wire lengths together. Thread several beads onto each length of wire, then twist wire lengths together; continue adding beads and twisting wire. Twist and curl remaining ends together to secure beads. Arrange beaded wire on table.

PAINTED WINE GLASSES

(shown on page 33)

For each glass, you will need rubbing alcohol, cotton balls, wine glass, lime green and green permanent enamel paint, round foam paintbrushes, and clear acrylic spray sealer.

Use alcohol in a well-ventilated area. Several coats of paint may be necessary for desired coverage. Allow paint and sealer to dry after each application.

1. Use alcohol and cotton balls to clean outside of glass.
2. Paint green dots on bottom of glass. Apply two coats of sealer.
3. Paint entire bottom of glass lime green. Apply two coats of sealer.

PAINTED CHARGERS
(shown on page 33)

For each charger, you will need rubbing alcohol; cotton balls; painter's masking tape; 13" dia. clear glass plate; lime green, teal, and green permanent enamel paint; paintbrushes; and clear acrylic spray sealer.

Use alcohol in a well-ventilated area. Several coats of paint may be necessary for desired coverage. Allow paint and sealer to dry after each application.

1. Use alcohol and cotton balls to clean outside of plate.
2. Enlarge package pattern, page 175, 137%, then tape pattern to front of plate. Use paint to lightly outline bow pattern on plate bottom. Paint bow lime green. Apply two coats of sealer.
3. Mask off area around package. Paint package teal; when dry, remove tape. Apply two coats of sealer.
4. Paint remainder of plate bottom apple candy green; when dry, apply two coats of sealer. Remove pattern.

ORNAMENTAL TABLE DÉCOR
(shown on page 34)

You will need a tablecloth, rubber bands, 1¹/₂"w wire-edged ribbon, floral wire, wire cutters, and 2¹/₂" dia. glass ornaments.

1. Gather each corner of tablecloth with a rubber band.
2. Tie a ribbon bow around gathered corners to cover rubber band.
3. For each corner, wire three ornaments together tightly; wrap wire around gathered corner and twist wire ends together to secure.

PAINTED ORNAMENTS
(shown on page 31)

You will need 3" dia. clear glass ornaments with metal end caps, green acrylic paint, matte medium, and small plastic cups.

1. Remove end caps from ornaments. Mix paint with matte medium until a thin consistency is achieved. Pour paint mixture into ornaments.
2. Covering opening with a paper towel, swirl paint mixture around, coating insides of ornaments.
3. To drain excess paint, place ornaments upside down in cups. Once excess paint has drained, place ornaments on their sides, with openings facing a fan until dry.
4. Carefully replace end caps.

FLOCKED ORNAMENTS
(shown on page 31)

You will need 3" dia. turnip-shaped or round clear glass ornaments with metal end caps, green acrylic paint, matte medium, small plastic cup, flocking kit (our kit includes flocking adhesive and assorted colors of flocking fibers), paintbrushes the width of desired stripes, craft glue, green glitter, decorative fiber trim, and clear self-adhesive paper.

Swirl

1. Follow Steps 1 – 4 of Painted Ornaments to paint ornament.
2. For each flocked stripe, follow manufacturer's instructions and use a paintbrush to apply a ¹/₄"w diagonal stripe of flocking adhesive to ornament; add fibers (we mixed green and turquoise fibers to get the color we desired). Once dry, remove excess fibers.
3. For each glitter stripe, use a paintbrush to apply a 1"w stripe of craft glue to ornament (we made our stripe thinner at the top and bottom of our ornament). While glue is still wet, sprinkle glitter over glue; allow to dry. Once dry, shake off any excess glitter.
4. Glue a length of fiber trim around top of ornament.

Loop

1. Follow Steps 1 – 4 of Painted Ornaments to paint ornament.
2. Trace loop pattern, page 175, onto self-adhesive paper; cut out. Adhere pattern to center of ornament.

3. Draw around pattern with a pencil; remove pattern, then repeat around ornament.

4. Working on one loop at a time and following manufacturer's instructions, apply flocking adhesive inside pattern lines. Add green fibers; once dry, remove excess fibers.

5. Apply a circle of glue around top of ornament; while glue is still wet, sprinkle glitter over glue; allow to dry. Repeat for bottom of ornament. Once dry, shake off any excess glitter.

BEAD-WRAPPED ORNAMENTS
(shown on page 31)

For each ornament, you will need a 4" dia. frosted glass ornament with metal end cap, blue-green acrylic paint, matte medium, small plastic cup, tape, medium-gauge silver craft wire, wire cutters, and assorted shades of green beads.

1. Follow Steps 1 – 4 of Painted Ornaments, page 140, to paint ornament.
2. For beading, tape ten 20" lengths of wire side-by-side to work surface.
3. Thread several beads onto each wire, then join two wires with a bead. Continue adding beads and joining different wires with a bead until beaded wires reach 12".
4. Being careful not to lose any beads, wrap wire ends with tape.
5. Wrap beaded wires around ornament, then remove tape and twist wire ends together to secure.
6. Stretch and shape wires at top and bottom to cover ornament.

BEAD-WRAPPED CANDLES
(shown on page 35)

You will need tape, medium-gauge green and silver craft wire, wire cutters, assorted shades of green beads, 4"h square and 6"h round green candles.

Never leave a burning candle unattended. For larger or smaller candles, simply adjust the number and length of wires.

1. Follow Steps 2 – 4 of Bead-Wrapped Ornaments, using six 15" lengths each of green and silver wire for square candles and nine 15" lengths each of green and silver wire for round candles.
2. Wrap the beaded wire around the candle, then remove tape and twist wire ends together to secure.

LIGHTED STAINED GLASS PANEL
(shown on page 35)

You will need rubbing alcohol, cotton balls, stained glass cobbles and mosaic stained glass squares in shades of green, 11$\frac{1}{2}$" x 18" beveled glass piece with rounded sides for background, 11"h square glass vase, glass adhesive, simulated black liquid leading, $\frac{1}{4}$"w silvered copper foil tape, brayer, painter's masking tape, sand, and a candle or tree lights.

Never leave a burning candle unattended.

1. Use alcohol and cotton balls to clean all stained glass pieces, background piece, and vase.

2. Draw around background piece onto white paper for outline.
3. Arrange stained glass pieces on paper, as desired, for design.
4. Starting at center, follow manufacturer's instructions to glue the glass pieces to background piece. Allow to cure.
5. Follow manufacturer's instructions to fill spaces between stained glass with leading. Wipe away any excess leading, then allow to cure.
6. Wrap edges of stained glass piece with foil tape; roll with brayer to adhere.
7. Matching bottom edges, glue stained glass piece to one side of vase. Use masking tape to secure pieces together until glue has cured.
8. Pour sand in vase for weight. Place candle or tree lights in vase.

SUSPENDED WREATH
(shown on page 34)

You will need a hot glue gun; 20" dia. foam wreath; lime green, teal, and two-toned green fabric; assorted shades and widths of green ribbon, including 1$\frac{1}{2}$"w wire-edged green ribbon; medium-gauge craft wire; wire cutters; assorted shades and sizes of green beads; floral pins; flocking kit (our kit includes flocking adhesive and assorted colors of flocking fibers); assorted shades of green ornaments (we followed Steps 1 and 2 of Swirl Flocked Ornament, page 140, and assorted colors of green paint to create some of our ornaments); T-pins; and 1$\frac{1}{2}$" dia. green metallic pom-poms.

1. Securing to the wreath with hot glue, wrap wreath with lime green fabric, ribbons, then teal and two-toned fabrics.
2. For each beaded garland, twist ends of two wire lengths together. Thread several beads onto each length of wire, then twist wire lengths together; continue adding beads and twisting wire. Twist and curl remaining ends together to secure beads. Securing ends with floral pins, wrap garland around wreath. Repeat for additional garlands as needed.
3. For flocked ribbon, use a pencil to draw polka dots on three 76" lengths of green ribbon. Following manufacturer's instructions, apply flocking adhesive over dots. Add green fibers; once dry, remove excess fibers.
4. To hang, thread flocked ribbon lengths around wreath at equal distances, then, leaving 4" streamers, gather ribbon ends and knot. Notch streamers.
5. Thread assorted ribbon lengths through each ornament hanger. Insert a T-pin through ribbon ends, then insert into wreath (we inserted our pin under the fabric to conceal the pin where possible).
6. Glue pom-poms to ribbon.

SQUARE ORNAMENT WREATH
(shown on page 30)

You will need four 24" stretcher bars, wood glue, two sheets of floral foam, serrated knife, green mylar, staple gun, assorted sizes and shades of green ornaments (we used approximately 200 ornaments ranging in size from 1" to 4" in diameter), medium-gauge craft wire, wire cutters, and wooden floral picks.

1. Glue stretcher bars together to make a square frame; allow to dry.
2. Glue foam sheets, side-by-side, to frame; allow to dry.
3. Using the serrated knife, trim foam even with outside edge of frame. Cut out center of wreath 4" from outside edge.
4. Wrap wreath loosely with mylar, stapling in place as necessary.
5. Thread 4" dia. ornaments onto lengths of wire; wrap each wire around frame, then twist wire ends together to secure.
6. For remaining ornaments, thread ornaments onto pick wire; twist wire ends to secure, then insert pick into foam. (We divided our ornaments into four groups by size, then arranged from largest to smallest.)
7. Insert small mylar squares between ornaments to fill any empty spaces.

KNIT CUFF STOCKINGS
(shown on page 30)

For each stocking, you will need tracing paper; 1/4 yd green fabric for stocking; paper-backed fusible web; assorted embellishments, including ribbons, 1" dia. velvet circles, decorative fiber trim, beads, sequins, and green metallic pom-poms; fabric glue; 1/4 yd fabric for lining; one skein of Lion Brand Fun Fur #3611 Citrus; one skein of Lion Brand Fun Fur #2590 Peacock; one skein of Lion Brand Homespun #369 Florida Keys Green; and size 35 straight knitting needles.

Use a 1/2" seam allowance for all sewing.

1. Extending sides to obtain desired length (we extended the pattern 21" to make a 30"-long stocking), trace stocking pattern, page 176, onto tracing paper; cut out.
2. Use pattern to cut out front and back stocking pieces (one in reverse).
3. For stocking front, use fusible web to attach ribbons, velvet circles, and trim. Leaving 1/2" along outside of stocking for seam allowance, sew beads and sequins in place. Use fabric glue to adhere pom-poms in place; allow to dry.
4. Matching right sides and leaving top edges open, sew stocking pieces together. Clip curves and turn right side out.
5. Use pattern to cut out front and back lining pieces (one in reverse). Matching right sides and leaving top edges open, sew lining pieces together. Clip curves; do not turn right side out. With wrong sides together and matching side seams, insert lining into stocking. Baste lining to stocking along top edges.
6. For cuff, leaving long tails of yarns at the beginning of stitches for finishing, hold one strand of each yarn together and cast on 8 stitches. Knit each row until cuff measures approximately 12", ending at same edge as beginning end. Bind off all stitches, leaving long tails at the ends of stitches for finishing.
7. Matching right sides and placing the opening at the heel side seam, place cuff inside stocking. Easing knit edge to fit, sew end of rows on cuff to top of stocking. Turn cuff to outside of stocking.
8. Using the long tails at bottom of cuff, whipstitch back seam.
9. Form loop with long tails at top of cuff and knot in place at inside of stocking. Glue knot to stocking; allow to dry, then cut off excess ends.

HARLEQUIN TREE SKIRT

(shown on page 31)

You will need butcher paper, ½ yd each of four shades of green fabric, two skeins of Lion Brand Fun Fur #3611 Citrus, two skeins of Lion Brand Fun Fur #2590 Peacock, one skein of Lion Brand Homespun #369 Florida Keys Green, size 35 straight knitting needles, 1" dia. velvet circles, green metallic pom-poms, and fabric glue.

Use a ½" seam allowance for all sewing.

1. Refer to Diagram to draw pattern on butcher paper. Cut out pattern ½" outside drawn lines for seam allowances.
2. Use pattern to cut four sections from each color fabric.
3. Matching long edges and right sides and alternating colors, sew sections together, leaving two long edges unsewn to create an open-ended skirt. Press all raw edges ½" to wrong side; topstitch.
4. For knit edging, hold one strand of each yarn together and cast on 3 stitches.
5. Knit each row until trim measures approximately 7 yards. Alternate the direction you turn the needles after every row to prevent the garland from twisting.

6. Bind off all stitches.
7. Using sewing needle and thread, sew end of rows on trim to edge of tree skirt, easing knit edge to fit.
8. Use fusible web to attach velvet circles. Use fabric glue to adhere pom-poms in place; allow to dry.

Diagram

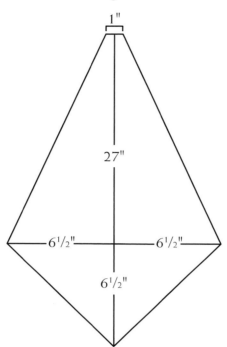

1"

27"

6½"　　6½"

6½"

KNIT GARLAND

(shown on page 29)

You will need two skeins of Lion Brand Fun Fur #3611 Citrus, two skeins of Lion Brand Fun Fur #2590 Peacock, one skein of Lion Brand Homespun #369 Florida Keys Green, and size 35 straight knitting needles.

1. Holding one strand of each yarn together, cast on 3 stitches.
2. Knit each row until garland measures approximately 5 yards or until Fun Fur is gone. Alternate the direction you turn the needles after every row to prevent the garland from twisting.
3. Bind off all stitches.

Yuletide Fiesta

FRUIT ORNAMENTS
(shown on page 39)

You will need assorted pony beads, fruit picks with wire stems, needle-nose pliers, embroidery floss, and craft glue.

1. Thread beads onto pick wire. Use pliers to loop end of wire to secure beads.
2. For hanger, knot ends of a 7" length of floss around fruit stem; trim ends. Add a dot of glue to knot.

NAPKINS AND NAPKIN RINGS
(shown on page 38)

You will need rickrack, fabric napkins, assorted buttons, assorted pony beads, fruit picks with wire stems, needle-nose pliers, and sprigs cut from an artificial greenery spray.

Napkins

1. Beginning at one corner, sew rickrack along outer edges of each napkin.
2. Sew a grouping of buttons at each corner of napkin.

Napkin Rings

1. Thread beads onto pick wire. Use pliers to loop end of wire to secure beads.
2. Wrap a piece of greenery around wire at base of fruit.
3. Loop wire around napkin.

CHALKBOARD PLATE
(shown on page 38)

You will need blackboard spray paint, 6½" dia. wooden disk, glue for wood and glass, 10½" dia. glass plate, dishtowel, three fruit picks with wire stems, nylon potholder loops, hot glue gun, and a plate stand.

Use spray paint in a well-ventilated area.

1. Paint front and sides of wooden disk; allow to dry.
2. Glue disk to center of plate.
3. For bow, cut a 5" x 12" strip from dishtowel. Fold each long edge to center on wrong side. Fold and overlap each end at center back. Gathering at center, wrap fruit pick stems around dishtowel.
4. Wrap and hot glue potholder loops around center of bow to hide wires. Hot glue bow to plate.
5. Display plate on stand.

YULETIDE WREATH
(shown on page 37)

You will need fruit picks with wire stems, 10" dia. artificial succulent wreath (we used a hen and chick wreath), dishtowel, assorted colors of yarn, ribbon, and a suction cup hanger (optional).

1. To secure fruit picks to wreath, wrap pick wires around bases of hens and chicks.
2. For bow, cut a 12" x 15" strip from dishtowel. Fold each long edge to center on wrong side. Fold and overlap each end at center back. Gathering at center, wrap bow with three lengths of yarn, leaving two long tails.
3. Use ends of yarn to tie bow to top of wreath.
4. For hanger, wrap a length of ribbon around wreath and knot ends together. (We used a suction cup hanger to attach the wreath to our window.)

TEA TOWEL TABLE RUNNER
(shown on page 38)

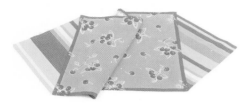

You will need two coordinating 18½" x 27" tea towels.

1. For end pieces, refer to Fig. 1 to cut corners from one towel at 14".

Fig. 1

2. Refer to photo to sew corner pieces to ends of remaining towel.

MATCHSTICK ORNAMENTS
(shown on page 39)

For each ornament, you will need eight kitchen matches, acrylic paint, wax paper, hot glue gun, three colors of yarn, embroidery floss, one button, and one pony bead.

1. Strike matches, then blow out to eliminate fire hazard. When cool, dip match tips in paint; allow to dry.
2. To form star shape with matches, arrange matches on waxed paper, then hot glue ends together. Allow glue to cool before removing star.

3. Starting at center of star, hot glue end of yarn to back of one match, then wrap yarn around match once. Wrapping yarn around each match in the same direction and changing yarn colors as desired, wrap yarn around star until you reach match tips. Hot glue yarn end to back of last match to secure.
4. For hanger, glue ends of a 9" length of floss to back of one match.
5. Hot glue button and bead to center front of ornament.

FIESTA LAMP
(shown on page 39)

You will need acrylic paint, paintbrush, display lamp kit, dishtowel, craft glue, 8¼"h x 10¼"w square lampshade, clothespins, jumbo rickrack, and a pitcher to fit on base.

1. Paint lamp base; allow to dry. Assemble lamp kit.
2. Cut two corners from towel. Folding as necessary, glue cut edges of corner pieces to inside top of lampshade at opposite sides. Use clothespins to hold towel pieces in place until glue dries.
3. Glue rickrack along bottom edges of lampshade.
4. Place pitcher on lamp base.

TIP: Use Tacky Wax® to secure your pitcher to the lamp base, without permanently damaging the pitcher.

LOOP GARLAND
(shown on page 39)

You will need a bag of nylon potholder loops.

1. Overlap two sets of loops (Fig. 1).

Fig. 1

2. Refer to Fig. 2 to join loops.

Fig. 2

3. Pull ends of loops to secure.
4. Repeat Steps 1 – 3 until desired length is achieved.

POT HOLDER CONES

(shown on page 39)

For each ornament, you will need a pot holder loom, three colors of yarn (we used light green sport weight yarn and red and yellow worsted weight yarn), crochet hook, chenille stem, assorted beads, and cardboard.

Figs. are shown using only one strand of yarn for clarity.

1. With notched side of loom at bottom, slip-knot ends of two skeins of yarn around peg at top right hand corner. Referring to Fig. 1, wrap yarn around pegs. Slip-knot yarn again around notched peg at bottom left hand corner. Do not cut yarn.

Fig. 1

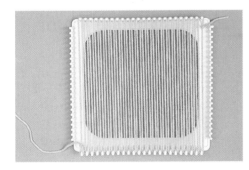

2. Referring to Fig. 2 and beginning with second notched peg, push yarn on every other peg to bottom notch; be sure to raise yarn on remaining pegs to top notch.

Fig. 2

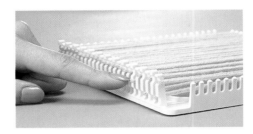

3. Bring yarn ends at bottom left notched peg up and around first peg on bottom left side of loom. Referring to Fig. 3 and using a crochet hook, weave yarn, over and under, across loom. Continue across loom to weave pot holder.

Fig. 3

4. To finish edges, refer to Fig. 4a and insert hook through loop 1, then catch and pull loop 2 through loop 1. With hook through loop 2, catch and pull loop 3 though loop 2. Continue in this manner along edges of pot holder (Fig. 4b) until reaching last loop. Knot last loop around itself.

Fig. 4a

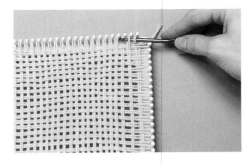

Fig. 4b

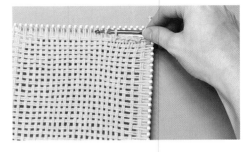

5. To form cone, use one strand of yarn to stitch two adjacent sides together.

6. For flap, turn down point to front of cone.

7. For hanger, thread one end of an $8^{1}/_{2}$" length of chenille stem though cone where flap starts; twist chenille stem around itself to secure. Thread beads onto stem. Thread remaining end through cone at opposite side; wrap stem around itself to secure.

8. Using yarn and a $1^{5}/_{8}$" cardboard square, follow *Making Tassels*, page 185, to make bottom tassel. Thread one bead onto tassel, then tie tassel to bottom of cone.

9. For flap beads, thread two beads onto a length of yarn. Double back through first bead, then tie beads to tip of flap.

Resplendent in Red

AMARYLLIS ARRANGEMENT

(shown on page 41)

You will need a large clear glass vase, assorted sizes of paintbrushes, assorted shades of red glass paint, floral wire, wire cutters, silk amaryllis stems, 1¹/₂"w red silk ribbon, and red and white marbles.

1. For vase, use ends of paintbrush handles to paint red dots on vase; allow to dry.
2. For arrangement, use floral wire to hold several amaryllis stems together. Tie a length of ribbon into a bow around stems to cover wire.
3. Place arrangement in center of vase, then add marbles to vase to secure arrangement.

RIBBON-STRIPED TABLE RUNNERS

(shown on page 42)

For each table runner, you will need two coordinating fabrics for

runner top and bottom (we used an orange-red fabric for the top and a dark red fabric for the bottom); assorted widths, textures, and shades of red ribbon; fabric marking pen; seed beads; sequins; and two beaded tassels.

Use a ¹/₂" seam allowance for all sewing.

1. Measure table to determine length and width of table; add the desired drop length to each end.
2. Cut a piece of each fabric the desired width for table runner top and bottom.
3. Cut assorted ribbons the length of the top piece. Position ribbon on right side of fabric. Baste ribbon ends in place along each end.
4. Fold ends of top and bottom to wrong side into a point, then press; mark stitching lines along folds on wrong side of fabric with pen.
5. Matching right sides, leaving an opening on one side for turning, and sewing points along stitching lines, sew top runner piece to bottom runner piece.
6. Cut off excess fabric at points, clip corners, then turn runner right side out. Sew opening closed; press.
7. Position sequins along ribbons, then, with a seed bead at center of each sequin and working through all layers of runner, sew sequins to runner and knot ends. Sew one tassel to each point.

ORANGE-RED GLASS ORNAMENTS

(shown on page 43)

For each ornament, you will need a 4" dia. clear glass ornament with metal end cap, orange-red acrylic paint, matte medium, and a small plastic cup.

1. Remove end cap from each ornament. Mix paint with matte medium until a thin consistency is achieved. Pour paint mixture into ornament.
2. Covering opening with a paper towel, swirl paint mixture around, coating inside of ornament.
3. To drain excess paint, place ornament upside down in cup. Once excess paint has drained, place ornament on its side, with opening facing a fan until dry.
4. Carefully replace end cap.

FABRIC-COVERED CANVAS ORNAMENTS

(shown on page 43)

You will need 3" x 4" wrapped canvases; hot glue gun; assorted colors and textures of red fabric; assorted widths, textures, and shades of red ribbon; bead glue; red sequins; and red beads.

1. Wrapping and hot gluing edges to back, cover canvases with desired fabric.
2. For striped ornaments, wrapping ends to back, hot glue ribbons to ornament.
3. For beaded ornaments, use bead glue to adhere sequins and beads to ornament.
4. For each hanger, knot ends of a length of ribbon together. Hot glue knot to top back of ornament.

POLKA-DOTTED ORNAMENTS

(shown on page 43)

For each ornament, you will need assorted sizes of round foam paintbrushes, assorted shades of red glass paint, 3" dia. red glass ornament with metal end cap, and $^1/_4$"w red satin ribbon.

1. Paint assorted sizes of red dots on ornament.
2. For hanger, thread a length of ribbon through end cap and knot ends of ribbon together.

DOTTED AND STRIPED CANDLEHOLDERS

(shown on page 43)

You will need assorted sizes of round and flat foam paintbrushes, assorted shades of red glass paint, assorted clear glass candleholders, painter's tape, and clear gloss glaze glass sealer.

Never leave burning candles unattended. Several coats of paint may be necessary for desired coverage.

1. For dotted candleholders, paint assorted sizes of red dots on candleholders.
2. For striped candleholders, use painter's tape to mask areas on candleholders. Paint candleholders; allow to dry. Remove tape.
3. Apply sealer.

FLOOR CUSHIONS

(shown on page 44)

For each cushion, you will need $1^1/_3$ yds of fabric, two $87^1/_2$" lengths of $^3/_8$" dia. cording, batting, 22" square of 4" thick foam, five $1^3/_4$" dia. buttons from a covered button kit, upholstery needle, heavy-duty thread, and five 1" dia. buttons for cushion back.

Use a $^1/_2$" seam allowance for all sewing.

1. Cut two 23" squares from fabric for cushion top and bottom. Follow *Welting*, pages 186 – 187, to make and attach a length of welting to cushion top and bottom.
2. Piecing as necessary, cut one 5" x $87^1/_2$" strip from fabric for cushion sides. Matching right sides, sew ends together; press seam to one side.
3. Placing seam at center bottom and matching raw edges, pin strip along edges of cushion front; sew strip in place. Leaving one end open for turning and inserting foam, pin, then sew side strip to cushion back. Clip corners and turn cushion right side out.
4. Cover foam with batting and loosely baste in place. Insert foam into cover, then sew opening closed.

5. Follow manufacturer's instructions to cover the $1^3/_4$" buttons with fabric. To tuft cushion, begin on bottom side of cushion and use the upholstery needle and heavy-duty thread to sew through a 1" button, up through cushion, through the covered button, then back down through the cushion and the 1" button; repeat. Pull threads and tightly knot together to secure. Repeat with remaining buttons.

FABRIC-COVERED BOXES

(shown on page 44)

You will need assorted sizes of papier-mâché boxes with lids (we used oval, round, square, and hexagonal boxes); assorted shades and textures of red fabric; spray adhesive; fabric glue; hot glue gun; clothespins; assorted widths, textures, and shades of red ribbon; beaded trim; jewel glue; assorted sizes and colors of faceted acrylic jewels; and a nail.

Use spray adhesive in a well-ventilated area. Use spray adhesive for gluing fabric to box, use fabric glue for gluing ribbon and edges of fabric, and use hot glue for any areas needing a stronger hold. Use clothespins to hold fabric and ribbon in place until glue dries.

1. To cover each box with fabric, measure height of box, then measure around box; add 1" to each measurement. Cut a fabric strip the determined size. Press and glue one end of strip ¹/₂" to wrong side.

2. Leaving ¹/₂" of fabric extended at top and bottom and overlapping ends at back, adhere fabric to box. Folding and clipping as needed, glue fabric edges to bottom and inside box.

3. For box bottom, draw around box on wrong side of fabric; cut out ¹/₂" outside drawn lines. Clipping edges as necessary, press fabric edges ¹/₂" to wrong side. Adhere fabric to box bottom.

4. To cover a lid, draw around top of lid on wrong side of fabric. Measure height of lid and add ¹/₂" to measurement. Cut out fabric the determined measurement outside the drawn lines. Folding fabric at corners, clipping edges as necessary, and gluing excess to inside of lid, adhere fabric to lid.

5. Wrapping ends to inside and bottom as necessary and gluing in place, glue ribbon and beaded trim to box or lid, if desired. Glue a length of ribbon along inside box or lid to cover ribbon ends.

6. Use jewel glue to add jewels to box.

7. For handle, use a nail to poke a hole in center of lid. Thread ends of a ribbon length through hole and knot ends inside lid.

Geometric Paintings
(shown on page 45)

For each painting, you will need a 12" x 36" piece of mat board, painter's tape, four shades of red acrylic paint, paintbrushes, and a frame to fit painting.

Several coats of paint may be necessary for desired coverage. Allow paint to dry between each application.

1. Referring to the Painting Diagram and using a yardstick, lightly mark pattern lines on mat board.

Painting Diagram

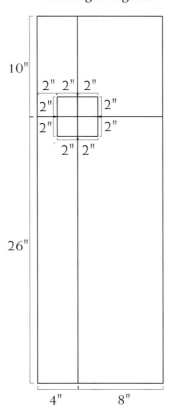

2. Mask around one section to be painted; paint section and allow it to dry. Remove tape. Mask around next section to be painted. Continue until all sections are painted.

3. Secure painting in frame.

Red Wreath
(shown on page 45)

You will need a hot glue gun, 20" dia. foam wreath, 2³/₄"w red silk ribbon, large and small silk poinsettia picks (we used approx. one bush each) and silk amaryllis (we used approx. five stems with three flowers each), and 2³/₄"w dark red wire-edged ribbon.

1. Hot gluing ends to secure, wrap wreath in silk ribbon.

2. Disassemble large poinsettias and amaryllis, then hot glue poinsettia and amaryllis petals (in one direction) to wreath, covering front and sides.

3. Spacing evenly around wreath, hot glue small amaryllis to wreath.

4. To hang, thread wire-edged ribbon through wreath, then tie ribbon length into a knot leaving two equally long ends. Tie ends into a bow.

ROUND SEQUINED PILLOW

(shown on page 45)

You will need two 18" squares of red silk fabric, assorted red sequins and beads, 16" dia. pillow form, and decorative trim.

Use a ¹/₂" seam allowance for all sewing.

1. Follow *Making a Fabric Circle*, page 186, using the fabric squares and 8¹/₂" between the string and the pencil, to make two fabric circles for pillow front and back.
2. Leaving 4" along outside of pillow front for seam allowance and trim, sew sequins and beads to pillow front.
3. Matching right sides and leaving an opening for inserting pillow form, sew pillow front to pillow back; clip curves. Turn pillow right side out, then insert pillow form; sew opening closed.
4. Sew trim along pillow front, 2" from seam.

TUFTED PILLOWS

(shown on page 45)

For each pillow, you will need ³/₈" dia. cording, fabric to cover cording and button, two 17" squares of fabric for pillow front and back, 16" square pillow form, 1¹/₂" dia. button from a covered button kit, upholstery needle and heavy-duty thread, and a 1" dia. button for pillow back.

Use a ¹/₂" seam allowance for all sewing.

1. Follow *Welting*, pages 186 – 187, to make and attach a length of welting to pillow front.
2. Matching right sides and leaving one edge open for inserting pillow form, sew pillow front and back together.
3. Turn pillow right side out, insert pillow form, then sew opening closed.
4. Follow manufacturer's instructions to cover the 1¹/₂" button with fabric. To tuft pillow, begin on back side of pillow and use the upholstery needle and heavy-duty thread to sew through the 1" button, up through the pillow, through the covered button, then back down through the pillow and the 1" button; repeat. Pull the threads and tightly knot together to secure.

RED RIBBON-STRIPED PILLOW

(shown on page 45)

You will need red silk fabric; assorted widths, textures, and shades of red ribbon; and polyester fiberfill.

1. Cut two 13" x 22" pieces from fabric for pillow front and back.
2. Cut 13" lengths of ribbon. Spacing evenly across pillow front and matching raw edges and ribbon ends, baste ends of ribbons to pillow front. (We layered some of our ribbons.)

3. Matching right sides and raw edges and leaving an opening along one end for turning, sew pillow front to pillow back; clip corners. Turn pillow right side out, insert fiberfill, then sew opening closed.

RED THROW

(shown on page 45)

You will need fabric glue, coordinating velvet ribbons and beaded trim, and a red chenille throw.

Embellish one edge, opposite edges, or trim throw all the way around.

Folding and gluing ends to wrong side, use fabric glue to attach velvet ribbon along the edge of the throw. Glue a length of beaded trim just above the ribbon, then glue a darker red ribbon just above the beaded trim.

BLUE AND BRONZE ENTRY

BLUE ORNAMENTS

(shown on page 46)

For each ornament, you will need a 3¼" dia. clear glass ornament with metal end cap, blue acrylic paint, matte medium, and a small plastic cup.

1. Remove end cap from ornament. Mix paint with matte medium until a thin consistency is achieved. Pour paint mixture into ornament.
2. Covering opening with a paper towel, swirl paint mixture around, coating inside of ornament.
3. To drain excess paint, place ornament upside down in cup. Once excess paint has drained, place ornament on its side, with opening facing a fan until dry.
4. Carefully replace end cap.

EGG ORNAMENTS AND TOPPER

(shown on page 46)

You will need small and large papier-mâché eggs (ours measure 4"h and 9"h); sandpaper; tack cloth; rust-colored metallic spray primer; small and large silk magnolia leaves; blue, bronze, and gold acrylic paint; toothbrush; clear acrylic spray sealer; hot glue gun; sequin pins; medium-gauge floral wire; wire cutters; large nail; and a 15" length of ¼" dowel rod.

Use spray primer and sealer in a well-ventilated area.

Ornaments

1. Sand small eggs, then wipe with a tack cloth.
2. Prime eggs and tops of small leaves; follow *Spatter Painting*, page 186, to spatter eggs and leaves with blue, bronze, and gold. Apply sealer.
3. Hot glue leaves around bottom of each egg. Reinforce bases of leaves with pins.
4. For hangers, use wire end to make a hole in top of each egg. Wrap one end of wire around nail to coil. Glue coiled end in egg, then bend a loop in remaining wire end.

Topper

1. Use nail to poke hole in bottom of large egg. Insert and hot glue dowel in hole.

2. Using the large egg and large leaves, follow Steps 1 – 3 of Ornaments.
3. Glue an additional layer of leaves above first layer. Reinforce base of leaves with pins.
4. Insert dowel in hole at top of Ribbon Tree.

RIBBON TREES

(shown on page 47)

For each tree, you will need a 16" length of ¾" hard plastic pipe, dish soap, masking tape, 15"h x 14" dia. fiberglass planter, quick-drying concrete mix, 6' length of ½" steel pipe, gravel, 5' tomato cage, heavy-duty pliers, 7" dia. craft ring, medium-gauge galvanized wire, wire cutters, two 25" C7 white light bulb stringer sets, heavy-duty plastic sheeting, low-temperature glue gun, medium-gauge floral wire, 4 yds light blue sheer fabric, straight pins, heavy-duty light blue thread, 4 yds antique gold tulle, 3"w gold sheer wire-edged ribbon, pearl garland, 1½"w blue krinkle ribbon, ⅞"w brown wire-edged ribbon, gold berry spray garland, greenery stems, Blue Ornaments, Egg Ornaments and Topper, and purchased oval and snowflake ornaments.

continued on page 152

1. Coat plastic pipe with dish soap. Use tape to form a grid across planter to hold plastic pipe in place at center of planter. Place coated pipe in planter.

2. Follow manufacturer's instructions to mix concrete. Fill bottom 8" of planter with concrete and allow to set; remove tape and pipe.

3. Insert steel pipe into hole and fill planter with gravel. Working at narrow end of tomato cage, bend ends of wires to meet at center, then bend ends 3" down through center of cage. Place cage over pipe and insert bent ends in pipe.

4. Fit craft ring snugly over top of cage. Cut two 5' lengths of galvanized wire per section of cage (between the upright wires). Wrap wire ends around cage rings and craft ring (Fig. 1).

Fig. 1

5. Connect light strings, then string lights around inside of cage ending with plug at bottom of tree.

6. To stabilize tree, attach one end of a length of galvanized wire to bottom ring of cage, wrap wire around pipe, then attach remaining end to opposite side of ring; trim ends. Move a quarter turn around the ring and repeat.

7. Wrap plastic sheeting around tree frame; trim to fit and hot glue in place. Wrap floral wire around one end of sheer fabric; attach to top of tree and wrap in a spiral around tree from top to bottom. Pin fabric around bottom ring; trim excess, then whipstitch around ring, going through sheeting as you stitch. Tack fabric to vertical wires as needed.

8. Wrap floral wire around one end of tulle; secure wire to top of tree. Loosely twist tulle. Attach end of 3"-wide ribbon to top of tree; wrap ribbon around tulle. Wrap tulle and ribbon around tree; hot glue in place at bottom.

9. Securing with floral wire, wrap pearl garland, blue and brown ribbons, and berry garland around tree. Add greenery stems as desired. Decorate with ornaments and topper.

BERIBBONED WREATHS
(shown on page 47)

For each wreath, you will need straight pins, four 5" x 56" strips of batting, four 12" x 60" pieces of sheer light blue fabric, 7/8"w brown wire-edged ribbon, 3"w gold sheer wire-edged ribbon, 20" dia. plastic foam wreath, floral pins, gold berry spray garland, and 1"w light blue ribbon.

1. Using straight pins to secure ends, wrap batting strips, fabric strips, then brown and gold ribbons around wreath.

2. Using floral pins to secure ends at back, wrap berry garland around wreath.

3. Use light blue ribbon to make desired length hanger for wreath.

SHIMMERING SWAG
(shown on page 47)

You will need sheer light blue fabric, antique gold tulle, 3"w gold sheer wire-edged ribbon, two 25" C7 white light bulb stringer sets, medium-gauge floral wire, wire cutters, pearl garland, greenery stems, gold berry spray garland, Blue and Egg Ornaments, and purchased snowflake ornaments.

1. Tucking ends under, drape sheer fabric across top of door frame.

2. Loosely twist tulle. Wrap tulle and ribbon around fabric. Add lights to swag.

3. Using wire, arrange and attach pearl garland, greenery, berry garland, and ornaments to swag.

DICKENS ENTRY

OUTDOOR GIFT BOXES
(shown on page 51)

You will need spray primer, sandpaper, assorted sizes of wooden boxes, tack cloth, ivory spray paint, clear acrylic spray sealer, hot glue gun, assorted colors and sizes of wire-edged ribbon, and artificial greenery picks (optional).

Use spray primer, paint, and sealer in a well-ventilated area.

1. For each box, prime, then sand box; wipe box with tack cloth. Paint box, then apply sealer.
2. Hot gluing ends at bottom and crossing at top, wrap ribbons around box. Make a ribbon bow, then hot glue bow to top of box where ribbons overlap. Add greenery, if desired.

EVERGREEN WREATH
(shown on page 49)

You will need floral wire, wire cutters, artificial greenery picks, artificial berry picks, 30" dia. greenery wreath with pinecones, silk poinsettias, hot glue gun, 2"w wire-edged plaid ribbon, 2¹/₂" dia. gold ornaments, music rubber stamp, black ink pad, and 2⁵/₈"w white wire-edged ribbon.

1. Use wire to attach greenery and berry picks to wreath until desired look is achieved.
2. Use wire to attach a grouping of poinsettias to wreath.
3. Hot gluing ends at back, wrap wreath with plaid ribbon.
4. Use wire to attach ornaments.
5. Stamp white ribbon with music stamp. Once dry, knot ribbon at center, then use wire to attach ribbon to wreath behind poinsettias.

LANTERN LUMINARIES
(shown on page 51)

You will need a hot glue gun, artificial greenery with pinecones, 2"w wire-edged plaid ribbon, artificial berries, metal lanterns with glass sides and ring handles, and a candle to fit in each lantern.

Never leave burning candles unattended.

1. Arrange and hot glue greenery, ribbon, and berries to base of lantern.
2. Hot glue a cluster of greenery and berries to top of lantern.
3. Place candle in lantern.

WALL SCONCE SWAG
(shown on page 50)

You will need floral wire, wire cutters, two 18" artificial greenery picks, artificial holly berry greenery, black ink pad, music rubber stamp, 2⁵/₈"w white ribbon, and 2"w wire-edged plaid ribbon.

1. For the swag, use floral wire to connect the picks together at the top.
2. Use floral wire to attach additional berry greenery as desired.
3. Stamp white ribbon with music stamp.
4. Use floral wire to attach a plaid ribbon bow and stamped ribbon streamers at top of swag.

SWAG GARLAND
(shown on page 48)

You will need a long artificial greenery garland (it may be necessary to use floral wire to attach several lengths of garland together to achieve desired length), floral wire, wire cutters, artificial holly berry greenery, silk poinsettias, black ink pad, music rubber stamp, 2⁵/₈"w white ribbon, and 2"w wire-edged plaid ribbon.

1. Hang garland over door frame.
2. Use floral wire to attach berry greenery and poinsettias to garland as desired.
3. Stamp white ribbon with music stamp.
4. Use floral wire to attach plaid ribbon and stamped ribbon to one end of garland. Wrap ribbons around garland.

CAROLERS
(shown on page 50)

You will need one $3/4$" x $11^1/2$" x 5' board for each adult caroler, $3/4$" x $9^1/2$" x 4' board for boy, wax-free transfer paper, jigsaw, drill, saw, six 1" x $1/2$" x 24" lengths of wood for arms, three 1" x $1/2$" x 4' boards for stands, sandpaper, spray primer, assorted acrylic paints (we used black, nutmeg brown, camel, raw sienna, burnt umber, and skin tone), paintbrushes, clear acrylic spray sealer, light red chalk, $1^1/2$"-long 8x32 bolts with washers and wing nuts, clothing (see below), plastic bags, staple gun, three $1^1/2$" hinges, hammer, three eye screws, three 7" chain lengths, and three cup hooks.

Clothing for the carolers can be found at thrift stores. The man wears junior girl's size 12 clothing, with a size 3 girl's shoe. The woman wears junior girl's size 10. The boy wears boy's size 5 clothing, with a size 13 boy's shoe. Use spray primer and sealer in a well-ventilated area. Refer to Painting Techniques, pages 185 – 186, before beginning project.

1. For tops of heads, mark man's board at 56", woman's board at 53", and boy's board at 43". Enlarge patterns, pages 178 – 180, as indicated on pattern pieces. Aligning tops of heads with marks on boards, transfer pattern outlines to boards.
2. Follow Leg Diagram and use jigsaw to cut out legs on man and boy. Cut around heads and shoulders. Drill a $1/4$" hole through shoulders $3/4$" from each edge.

Leg Diagram

25$^1/2$" man

20" boy

2" 2" 2" 2"

3. From arm pieces, cut four 12" lengths for each adult and four 9" lengths for boy. Drill a $1/4$" hole $3/4$" from both ends of each upper arm and through one end of each lower arm.
4. Cut woman's stand 45" long and boy's stand 38" long.
5. Sand and prime all wood pieces. Paint stands black. Paint heads and the front and back of neck areas with skin tone; apply sealer. Transfer pattern details to each head.
6. Refer to photo to paint facial features and hair. Apply sealer. Use a soft paintbrush to apply chalk to cheeks, chins, noses, and under eyebrows. Apply sealer.
7. Bolt upper arms to shoulders and lower arms to elbows.
8. Clothe the carolers, adding plastic bags to shape where needed. Tuck and staple clothing to fit.
9. For each stand, attach hinge to back of caroler's neck and to one end of stand. Attach eye screw and chain to back waist area of caroler. Lean caroler back slightly to desired position and attach cup hook to stand to hold chain taut.

WHIMSICAL DOOR WREATHS
(shown on page 53)

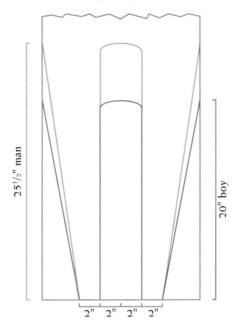

You will need medium-gauge craft wire, wire cutters, greenery garlands, two 7" dia. craft rings, hot glue gun, $2^1/2$"w yellow and white wire-edged ribbon, two 21" dia. artificial greenery wreaths, two 17" dia. artificial greenery wreaths, and 6"w red and white wire-edged ribbon.

1. For each small wreath, use wire to attach garland pieces to craft ring. Hot gluing ends at back of wreath, wrap wreath with yellow and white ribbon.
2. For each large and medium wreath, hot gluing ends at back of wreath, wrap wreath with yellow and white ribbon.
3. Hang red and white ribbon down center of each door; trim ends as desired. Evenly spacing, attach one of each size wreath to each ribbon.

RIBBON-TIED LUMINARIES
(shown on page 52)

For each luminary, you will need a 23" length of $2^1/2$"w yellow and white wire-edged ribbon, $7^1/2$" x $3^1/2$" dia. clear glass candleholder, artificial greenery picks, red and white swirled artificial berry picks, and a candle to fit candleholder.

Never leave burning candles unattended.

1. Using a square knot, tie ribbon around candleholder; trim ends. Slide greenery and berry picks behind knot.
2. Place candle in candleholder.

DOOR GARLAND WITH JUMBO ORNAMENTS

(shown on page 53)

You will need a long artificial greenery garland (it may be necessary to use floral wire to attach several lengths of garland together to achieve desired length); red, white, and green 1/4"-thick foam sheets; thin sheet of metal; tin snips; fabric glue; hammer and nail; hinged metal ring; floral wire; wire cutters; shiny red, shiny white, and matte green glass ball ornaments; and red and white swirled artificial berry picks.

Use caution when working with metal and tin snips.

1. Hang garland over door frame.
2. For ornaments, enlarge desired ornament pattern, pages 176 – 177, 168%; cut out. Draw around ornament on foam base color. Cut shapes from desired foam colors and cap from metal sheet. Glue shapes and cap on base piece.
3. Use hammer and nail to poke a hole through cap.
4. For hanger, thread ring through cap. Hang ornaments on garland.
5. Use floral wire to attach glass ornaments and berry picks to garland.

COLUMN GREENERY

(shown on pages 52 – 53)

For each column base arrangement, you will need a serrated knife; 20" dia. plastic foam wreath; artificial greenery picks; floral wire; wire cutters; shiny red, shiny white, and matte green glass ball ornaments; and red and white swirled artificial berry picks.

1. Use knife to cut wreath in half.
2. Add greenery picks to tops and sides of each wreath half until desired look is achieved.
3. Use floral wire to attach ornaments to wreath halves. Add berry picks.
4. Place wreath halves around base of column.

WREATH TOPIARIES

(shown on pages 52 – 53)

For each topiary, you will need 36" x 1³/₈" dia. dowel or curtain rod; 21" dia. artificial greenery wreath on wire frame; brown, light green, and red spray paint; clear acrylic spray sealer; terra cotta planter; medium-gauge galvanized wire; wire cutters; 2¹/₂"w yellow and white wire-edged ribbon; red and white swirled artificial berry picks; silicone sealer; 1¹/₂" dia. pipe adapter joint; plastic foam; and additional artificial greenery (we cut a section out of a wreath then coiled the wreath to fit in the planter).

Use spray paint, spray sealer, and silicone sealer in a well-ventilated area.

1. Insert rod between the wires of the wreath frame. Mark rod where wires touch. Remove rod, then cut 1/4" notches at marks.
2. Paint rod brown, then lightly paint green. Paint planter red. Apply sealer.
3. Reinsert rod into wreath, resting wreath in notches. Use pieces of wire to attach rod to wreath.
4. Beginning and ending at back of wreath, wrap wreath with ribbon. Add berry picks to wreath as desired.
5. Mark center bottom on inside of planter. Use silicone sealer to adhere pipe adapter joint at mark. Insert end of rod in adapter joint at center of planter.
6. Cut pieces of plastic foam to fit in top of planter to help secure rod.
7. Place a ring of greenery in top of planter.
8. Tie length of ribbon around planter.

Share the Spirit

FRAMED MEMORABILIA
(shown on page 61)

You will need an 11" x 14" frame; cardboard; assorted fabrics, handkerchiefs, and doilies; spray adhesive; hot glue gun; double-sided tape; vintage postcard; dimensional foam dots; coordinating cardstock; photographs; and embellishments (we used memorabilia, twine, stamped tags, metal frames and letters, buttons, and assorted die cuts).

Use spray adhesive in a well-ventilated area.

1. Remove glass and backing from frame. Draw around glass onto cardboard; cut out. For background, use spray adhesive to cover cardboard with fabric; wrap and glue fabric edges to back. Arrange and tape handkerchiefs and doilies on background.
2. Place background in frame. From the front, lightly mark along the inner edges of the frame on the fabric with a pencil. This defines your usable design area. Remove background from the frame.
3. Cut desired image from postcard. Use foam dots to mount image to cardstock; cut out 1/8" from image.
4. Working inside the usable design area, arrange and glue photographs, mounted image, and embellishments on background.
5. Place frame glass, background, and frame backing in frame. Arrange and glue embellishments on frame glass.

BEADED BROOCH
(shown on page 58)

You will need stiffened black felt, mint green seed beads, 1" and 1⅛" dia. white buttons, glass heart and  flower beads, black beading thread, beading needle, black felt, fabric glue, and a pin back.

1. Cut a 3" square of stiffened felt. Adding seed beads to thread as you sew on buttons, stack and sew buttons to center of square.
2. Adding seed beads to thread as you sew on flowers, sew glass beads around stacked buttons.
3. To add seed beads around glass beads, bring threaded needle up through felt where you want to start; add five seed beads to thread, lay beads along edges of glass beads, and sew down by bringing needle through to back of felt. Bring needle back up through felt between the second and third seed beads; sew down to secure beaded thread. Bring needle back up through felt between the fourth and fifth seed beads and take needle through fifth bead. Add three more seed beads to thread, lay beads along edges of glass beads, and sew down. Bring needle back up through felt between last two seed beads, then take needle through third bead and add on three more beads. Continue in this manner to sew seed beads around glass beads. At end, insert beading needle down through felt and secure.

4. For pin, trim felt away close to beads.
5. Glue a 1⅝" dia. circle of regular felt to back of pin. Sew pin back to circle.

BUTTON BRACELET
(shown on page 58)

Refer to Knit and Crochet Basics, page 187, before beginning project.

You will need one skein of Luster Sheen Yarn #805 Natural, size G (4mm) crochet hook, 1"w grosgrain ribbon, and assorted buttons.

Ch 7.

Row 1: Sc in second ch from hook and in each ch across: 6 sc.

Row 2: Ch 1, turn; sc in each sc across.

Repeat Row 2 until piece measures approximately 6½" (16.5 cm) from beginning ch.

Last Row: Ch 5, turn; skip first 5 sc, slip st in last sc; finish off.

Arrange and sew buttons on bracelet. Glue a 6½" length of ribbon to wrong side of bracelet for stability.

RIBBON-WRAPPED WREATH
(shown on page 59)

You will need a 18" dia. foam wreath, hot glue gun, cotton batting, assorted ribbons, beaded garland, handkerchief, and a decorative pin.

1. Gluing at back of wreath as necessary, wrap wreath with strips of batting, then lengths of ribbon and garland.
2. Fold handkerchief. Use decorative pin to pin a folded length of ribbon to handkerchief. Arrange and glue handkerchief on wreath.

CANDLE JARS
(shown on page 56)

You will need two candle jars (we used 5½"h x 4" dia. jars); black fine-point permanent marker; assorted green and red ribbons; Perfect Glue™ #1; snowflake charms; red Christmas fabric; assorted seed, bugle, and pearl beads; beading thread; and a beading needle.

Green Candle Jar

1. Measure ⅞" from top of jar; mark a parallel line around jar. Measure from line to center bottom of jar. Cut desired number lengths of assorted ribbons the determined measurement.
2. Aligning one end of ribbon with line, glue each ribbon length to jar, wrapping opposite end of length to bottom of jar.

3. Glue a length of ribbon around jar, covering marked line and ribbon ends.
4. Catching a charm in the knot, knot a length of ribbon around jar lid.

Red Candle Jar

1. Measure around the jar; add 1". For band, cut a 3" wide strip of fabric the determined length.
2. Press each long edge ¼" to the wrong side twice; topstitch.
3. Matching right sides and raw ends, fold band in half. Using a ½" seam allowance, sew ends together. Turn band right side out; press.
4. Sew beads to band to accent designs in fabric.
5. Catching a charm in the knot, knot a length of ribbon around jar lid.

BERIBBONED ORNAMENTS
(shown on page 57)

For each ornament, you will need a 3½" dia. glass ornament, craft knife, assorted ribbons/trims, hot glue gun, 1¼" dia. silver jingle bell, ¾" dia. flat bead, alphabet stickers, cream cardstock, two self-adhesive clear tags, and liquid fray preventative.

1. Remove end cap from ornament. Use craft knife to enlarge opening in end cap; set aside.
2. Cut five 20" lengths of assorted ribbons/trims. Set aside one ribbon length.

3. Fold one length of ribbon/trim in half to find center of length. Glue center of length to bottom of ornament. Stopping at "neck" of ornament, wrap and glue length up opposite sides of ornament. Crisscrossing at center bottom and spacing evenly around ornament, glue four ribbon/trim lengths to ornament.
4. Thread jingle bell onto center of reserved ribbon length. Thread length ends through bead. With ribbon ends apart, glue bead to center bottom of ornament. Stopping at "neck" of ornament, wrap and glue length up opposite sides of ornament.
5. Threading remaining ends of ribbon/trim pieces through opening in cap, carefully replace end cap.
6. Adhere stickers to cardstock; cut out close to stickers. Sandwich card stock piece between two tags. Slip knot a length of ribbon through hole in tag; tie ends around neck of ornament.
7. For hanger, thread a length of ribbon through end cap and knot ends of ribbon together, forming a loop.
8. Trim, then apply liquid fray preventative to all ribbon/trim ends.

APPLIQUÉD TEA TOWELS
(shown on page 60)

You will need 2 tea towels, tracing paper, paper-backed fusible web, fabric scraps, transfer paper, black embroidery floss, and assorted buttons.

continued on page 158

Refer to Embroidery Stitches, page 186, before beginning project.

1. Omitting pom-poms and Santa's nose, trace desired patterns, page 181, onto tracing paper; cut out. Turn traced patterns over to reverse patterns. Leaving ¹/₂" between pieces, draw around each pattern piece onto paper side of fusible web.
2. Follow manufacturer's instructions to fuse drawn patterns to wrong side of fabric scraps. Do not remove paper backing. Cut out appliqué pieces along drawn lines.
3. To transfer embellishment lines from tracing paper pattern, place transfer paper, coated side down, on right side of appliqué. Place tracing paper pattern over transfer paper and draw over detail lines with ballpoint pen that does not write or a dull pencil.
4. For each design, remove paper backing from appliqué pieces. With bottom of design approximately 2¹/₂" to 3" from one end of towel, arrange and fuse appliqué pieces to towel.
5. Using a medium-width zigzag stitch, machine satin stitch around all raw edges and detail lines on appliqués.
6. Using six strands of floss, work *French Knots* for Santa's eyes and mouth. Sew buttons on caps and for Santa's nose.

Santa Box
(shown on page 60)

You will need a 7"w x 9"h wooden box with lid; tracing paper; transfer paper; acrylic paints (we used red, blue, cream, green, pink, and yellow); paintbrushes; black fine-point permanent marker; craft glue; and clear glitter.

1. Trace Santa pattern, page 181, onto tracing paper. Transfer pattern to box.
2. Referring to photo, paint box and lid. Use end of paintbrush handle to paint yellow dots on box. Use marker to outline design.
3. Apply glue to desired areas. While glue is still wet, sprinkle areas with glitter; shake off excess glitter and allow to dry.

Framed Hankie
(shown on page 61)

You will need a 4³/₄" x 6¹/₄" frame, cardboard, spray adhesive, hankie, vintage postcard, coordinating cardstock, ¹/₄" dia. hole punch, embellishments (we used ribbons, buttons, and a postage stamp), and a hot glue gun.

Use spray adhesive in a well-ventilated area.

1. Remove glass and backing from frame. Draw around glass onto cardboard; cut out. For background, use spray adhesive to cover cardboard with hankie; wrap and glue edges to back.
2. Place background in frame. From the front, lightly mark along the inner edges of the frame on the fabric with a pencil. This defines your usable design area. Remove background from the frame.
3. Cut desired image from postcard. For tag, tape image to cardstock; cut out ¹/₈" from image. Punch a hole through top of tag. Slip knot a length of ribbon through hole.
4. Working inside the usable design area, arrange and glue tag and embellishments on background.

5. Place frame glass, background, and frame backing in frame. Arrange and glue embellishments on frame glass and around frame.

Knit Collars
(shown on pages 58 and 59)

Refer to Knit and Crochet Basics, page 187, before beginning project.

Finished Size: One Size Fits Most

You will need one skein of Bernat Boa #81530 Cardinal **or** one skein of Lion Brand Fun Fur #153 Black, size 13 (9mm) straight knitting needles, and a decorative pin.

Gauge: In pattern, 10 sts = 4" (10 cm)

Cast on 10 sts.

Rows 1-3: Knit across.

Row 4: K1, ★ YO (*Fig. 2, page 186*), K2 tog (*Fig. 1, page 186*); repeat from ★ across to last st, K1.

Rows 5-7: Knit across.

Row 8: K1, (YO, K2 tog) across to last st, K1.

Repeat Rows 5-8 until Collar measures approximately 18" (45.5 cm) from cast on edge, ending by working Row 7.

Bind off all sts in **knit**. Pin closed with decorative pin.

Wrap Up the Holidays

Cotton Batting Bags

(shown on page 64)

You will need cotton batting, greeting cards, coordinating ribbons, and embellishments (we used bells, candy cane buttons, and a snowflake die cut).

Use a ¼" seam allowance for all sewing.

1. Cut a 21" x 15½" piece, a 27" x 18½" piece, and a 32" x 20½" piece from batting.
2. For each bag, matching wrong sides and short edges, fold batting in half. Mark desired card placement, unfold batting, and use a zigzag stitch to attach card to front of bag.
3. Matching right sides and short edges, fold bag in half; sew side seams. Clip corners and turn bag right side out.
4. Fill bag and tie a ribbon bow around bag to close. Attach embellishments to bag.

Decorated Envelope

(shown on page 67)

You will need red cardstock; double-sided tape; red print and linen-look scrapbook papers; 10" x 13" white mailing envelope; red vellum; Christmas card; silver brads; brown chalk; two 3" tall tags; craft glue; ribbon scrap; metal Christmas tags; string; buttons; bells; "wish" charm; spiral paper clip; snowflake brad; medium-gauge silver wire, wire cutters, and needle-nose pliers (optional); and 1½"w striped ribbon.

1. Tear two 1½"w strips from cardstock. Layer and tape torn strips and red print paper on envelope; trim papers.
2. Cut and tear papers, vellum, and card as desired; arrange as desired and tape layers together. Use brads to attach papers to front of envelope.
3. Use chalk to shade edges of 3" tags. Decorate top tag with cardstock, ribbon scrap, metal tag, brads, string, buttons, and a bell. Write message on bottom tag.
4. Embellish envelope with metal tag, charm, paper clip, snowflake brad, and curled wire lengths if desired. Tie ribbon bow around envelope; tie tags and bells to bow.

Felt Bag

(shown on page 66)

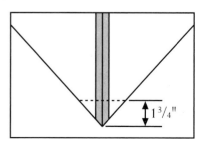

You will need ³⁄₈ yd of red wool felt; tracing paper; white, green, and gold felt scraps; red, white, and green embroidery floss; fabric glue; 10mm white pom-poms; flat red sequins; and white seed beads.

Use a ½" seam allowance for all sewing. Use two strands of floss for all embroidery stitches.

1. Cut a 10" x 26" piece from red felt. Fold short ends 1" to wrong side; topstitch along raw edges and folds.
2. With right sides together, sew side seams. For each mock box corner, refer to Fig. 1 to match side seam to fold along bottom of bag; sew across corner 1¾" from point. Turn bag right side out.

Fig. 1

1¾"

continued on page 160

3. For each handle, cut two 1" x 12" strips from red felt; stack and topstitch along long edges. Pin handle ends to inside top of bag; sew handle to bag.

4. Trace patterns, page 182, onto tracing paper; cut out. Using patterns, cut tree, ornaments, and star from felt scraps. Use green floss and a Running Stitch, page 186, to sew tree and star appliqués to bag front.

5. Glue ornaments and pom-poms to tree. Use red floss and a French Knot, page 186, to attach a sequin to each ornament. Use white floss to sew beads to tree.

EMBOSSED GIFT BAG AND TAG
(shown on pages 63 – 64)

You will need large, medium, and small snowflake rubber stamps; blue variegated and white ink pads; 8" x 10" brown gift bag with handles removed; clear and gold embossing powders; heat embossing tool; blue vellum; "Merry Christmas" rubber stamp; vellum tape; assorted ribbons; 1/4" dia. hole punch; deckle-edged scissors; brown and tan cardstock; and liquid fray preventative.

Use caution when working with the heat embossing tool.

1. Using large snowflake stamp and variegated ink, stamp snowflakes on bag. While wet, sprinkle clear embossing powder on stamped designs. Use heat embossing tool and follow manufacturer's instructions to heat-set designs. Repeat to stamp and emboss small and medium snowflakes on bag.

2. Tear a 4 1/2"w strip from vellum. Use white ink and stamp "Merry Christmas" on center of strip. Use gold embossing powder and emboss design. Use vellum tape to adhere vellum to bag front; trim ends of vellum.

3. For each handle, cut 28" lengths from two ribbons. Knot ribbons together at center, then 4" from center on each side. Thread ribbon ends through existing holes in bag or punch holes as needed; knot ends to secure.

4. For tag, use deckle-edged scissors to cut a 3 1/4" x 4 1/4" tag from brown cardstock and a 3" x 4" tag from tan cardstock; trim corners from one end.

5. Stamp and emboss large snowflake on tan tag; center and tape on brown tag. Punch hole through top of tag, then attach ribbons. Notch, then apply fray preventative to ribbon ends.

TWO-TAG GIFT HOLDER
(shown on page 67)

You will need two 2 3/8" x 4 3/4" manila tags, transparent and double-sided tapes, cotton swab, red chalk, red and cream cardstock, green handmade paper, deckle-edged scissors, red embroidery floss, hot glue gun, four small red buttons, small cellophane bag, and 1/4"w variegated green ribbon.

Use double-sided tape for all applications unless otherwise indicated.

1. For gift holder, use scissors to score each tag 1/2" from bottom end; fold along scored line, then unfold. Use transparent tape to tape bottom ends of tags together. Use cotton swab to apply chalk along edges of gift holder.

2. For label, cut a piece of red cardstock to fit front of gift holder. Tear a piece of handmade paper 1/8" smaller on all sides than cardstock. Machine sew paper to center of cardstock; tape cardstock to center of gift holder front.

3. Print messages on cream cardstock; use deckle-edged scissors to cut out. Use cotton swab to apply chalk along edges of messages. Tape messages to gift holder front. Taping ends to inside front of gift holder, wrap a length of floss around gift holder front. Hot glue a button in each corner of label.

4. Place gift in bag. Refold gift holder along scored lines. Tape bag to inside front and bottom of gift holder. Knot lengths of floss and ribbon through holes at top of gift holder.

FOLDED BOX
(shown on page 66)

You will need spray adhesive, 11" x 14" piece of Bristol board, gold swirl handmade paper, transfer paper, craft knife and cutting mat, craft glue, 7/8"w and 1 1/2"w sheer gold ribbons, pinking shears, gold scrapbook paper, diamond-shaped metal frame, 1/8" dia. hole punch, two 3/16" dia. gold brads, natural cardstock, gold paint pen, and an artificial berry sprig.

Use spray adhesive in a well-ventilated area.

1. Piecing as necessary and wrapping and gluing paper to the wrong side, use spray adhesive to cover Bristol board with handmade paper.
2. Use a photocopier to enlarge box pattern, page 183, 142%. Transfer box pattern to covered Bristol board.
3. Referring to pattern, use craft knife to cut out box along black lines. Being careful not to cut completely through board, use craft knife to score box along grey lines on pattern. Fold box along score lines. Overlap and glue side, then bottom edges together. Place gift in box. Fold top flap to back of box and secure in notch.
4. Overlapping ends at front of box, layer and glue ribbons around box. Trim ends as desired with pinking shears to prevent fraying.

5. For tag, cut a piece of scrapbook paper to fit in frame; glue behind frame. Punch a hole in each side of tag; insert brads in holes. Print "For You" on natural cardstock; cut into a small tag. Highlight small tag and berry sprig with paint pen. Arrange and glue small tag, then berry sprig at center of tag.

PINCH BOXES
(shown on page 66)

For each box, you will need tracing paper, template plastic, desired silk fabric, spray adhesive, red and green cardstock, craft glue, 1/16" dia. hole punch, three 1/8" dia. green eyelets, eyelet setter, one red or green "e" bead, 1/8"w red and green silk ribbons, 1 1/2" long red tassel, and decorative-edged craft scissors.

Use spray adhesive in a well-ventilated area.

1. Trace box pattern including dots, page 182, onto tracing paper; cut out. Draw around pattern three times on template plastic; cut out.
2. Cut a piece of fabric 1/2" larger on all sides than box pieces. Apply spray adhesive to wrong side of one fabric piece. Center and adhere one box piece to wrong side of fabric. Clip edges, then wrap fabric to wrong side of box piece. Repeat with remaining box and fabric pieces.
3. Cut three pieces of either red or green cardstock 1/8" smaller on all sides than box pieces. Center and glue one cardstock piece to wrong side of each box piece.
4. Referring to pattern for placement, punch holes along both edges of one box piece for bottom box piece. Punch holes along one edge only on each of the remaining two box pieces for side box pieces. Attach an eyelet, 1/4" from edge, in center of remaining side edges.
5. Thread "e" bead onto center of a 1 1/2 yard length of either red or green ribbon. Thread both ribbon ends through hole at one end of bottom box piece. Align punched edge of one side box piece with one punched edge of bottom piece. Working over, then under edges (similar to lacing a tennis shoe), use one ribbon end to lace edges together. Repeat with remaining side piece and ribbon end. Tie ribbon ends together at end of box sides. Knot ends together 2" from box; trim ends.
6. Thread loop of tassel through bottom holes in sides of box. Pass tassel through loop and cinch.
7. For tag, print "Do Not Open Until Christmas" onto green cardstock; use craft scissors to cut out. Attach an eyelet at top of tag. Thread a length of ribbon through eyelets in box. Thread one end of ribbon through eyelet in tag; tie ribbon ends into a bow to secure.

ORIGAMI BOXES

(shown on page 65)

For each box, you will need Bristol board, assorted scrapbook papers, spray adhesive, ruler, craft knife and cutting mat, and assorted embellishments to wrap gift and decorate box (we used tissue paper, assorted ribbons and tags, beaded wire, and stickers).

Use spray adhesive in a well-ventilated area.

1. For small box, cut one 6" square each from Bristol board and desired scrapbook paper. Use spray adhesive to adhere paper to one side of Bristol board.
2. Referring to Fig. 1, use a ruler to divide board piece into nine equal squares; lightly mark squares on wrong side of board.

Fig. 1

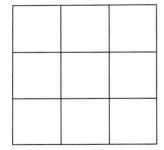

3. Use craft knife to cut corner squares from board piece. For box depth, refer to Fig. 2 and lightly mark a line ¼" away from center lines on each remaining side square. Being careful not to cut completely through board, use craft knife to score box along center lines and depth lines.

Fig. 2

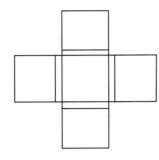

4. Cutting from depth line across to opposite corner, refer to Fig. 3 and cut triangles from side squares for flaps.

Fig. 3

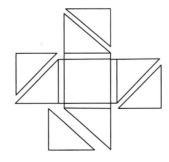

5. For medium box, repeat Steps 1-4 using a 9" square of Bristol board and ¾" for depth line measurement.
6. For large box, repeat Steps 1-4 using a 12" square of Bristol board and 1" for depth line measurement.
7. Wrap gift in tissue paper if desired. Place gift in center bottom of box. Refer to Fig. 4 to fold three flaps along score lines. Tuck fourth flap under folded flaps to secure.

Fig. 4

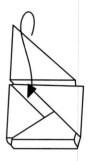

8. Refer to photo and embellish boxes as desired.

Merry Munchies to Share

COOKIE CARD
(shown on page 70)

You will need an 8¹/₂" x 11" sheet of white cardstock, assorted red and green scrapbook papers, decorative-edged craft scissors, craft glue, four ³/₁₆" dia. silver brads, embellishments to decorate card (we used alphabet stickers and spiral paper clips with beads and jingle bells threaded on the clips), double-sided tape, cellophane, and ¹/₄"w iridescent ribbon.

1. For card, matching short edges, fold cardstock sheet in half.
2. For card cover, matching short edges, fold a sheet of red paper in half. Using craft scissors as desired, cut one piece each of red and green paper. Glue green piece to front of cover. Use brads to attach red piece to front of cover. Embellish card cover. Glue card cover to outside of card.
3. Overlapping ends at back and securing with tape, wrap cookie in cellophane; secure ends with lengths of ribbon. Tape cookie to card.

WRAPPED MUG
(shown on page 70)

You will need a coffee mug; brown, off-white, and gold cardstock; scallop-edged scissors; striped vellum; craft glue; ¹/₁₆" dia. hole punch; eyelet setter; three ¹/₈" dia. gold eyelets; ³/₈"w red velvet ribbon; textured green scrapbook paper; alphabet stamp set; brown ink pad; red linen thread; dimensional foam dots; and a snowman sticker.

1. For sleeve, tear a piece of brown cardstock to fit around mug plus ¹/₂". Cut a piece of off-white cardstock the same size as brown cardstock; use scallop-edged scissors to trim ¹/₄" from each long edge. Cut a piece of vellum the same size as off-white cardstock; trim ¹/₄" from each long edge. Layer and glue pieces together.
2. For tabs, refer to Fig. 1 and cut corners from ends of sleeve. Center and attach an eyelet ¹/₄" from end of each tab.

Fig. 1

3. Overlapping tabs behind handle of mug, wrap sleeve around mug. Thread a length of ribbon through eyelets; tie ends into a bow.

4. For label, tear a piece of green scrapbook paper. Cut a piece of gold cardstock ¹/₄" smaller on all sides than green paper. Punch holes around edges of gold cardstock. Stamp "SPICED CIDER" on gold cardstock. Layer and glue pieces together. Center and attach an eyelet at one end of tag. Knot a length of linen thread through eyelet. Use foam dots to adhere snowman to label, then label to sleeve.

NUTCRACKER SWEETS CANISTER
(shown on page 71)

You will need a 9¹/₄"h x 3" dia. snack chip container with lid; white, black, cream, tan, red, and green cardstock; craft glue; tracing paper; ¹/₈" and ¹/₄" dia. hole punches; ³/₁₆" dia. gold trim; two ¹/₂" dia. wooden balls; cotton swab; red chalk; black fine-point permanent marker; artificial fur trim; and three ³/₁₆" dia. gold brads.

1. Remove container lid. Overlapping edges at back, glue a piece of green cardstock around container.
2. Trace patterns, page 184, onto tracing paper; cut out. Using patterns, cut pieces from cardstock. Punch ¹/₄" dia. pupils from black cardstock.

continued on page 164

3. Arrange and glue coat, belt, pants, and boots on container. Glue a length of gold trim across coat.

4. Overlapping edges at back, roll and glue each arm into a $1/2$" dia. tube. Glue a length of gold trim around each arm $1/2$" from top edge. For hands, glue wooden balls inside bottoms of arms. Arrange and glue arms on container.

5. Arrange and glue facial features on head. Use cotton swab to apply chalk for cheeks. Use marker to draw teeth. For hair, glue a length of fur trim along each side of head. Arrange and glue head on container. For beard, glue a length of fur trim below teeth.

6. Arrange and glue hat pieces together. Wrapping edges to back of hat, glue a length of trim across hat. Punch $1/8$" dia. holes in hat brim as shown on pattern. Punch three $1/8$" dia. holes in rim of container lid 2" apart. Aligning holes, use brads to attach hat to lid. Replace lid on container.

FUDGE BOX
(shown on page 72)

You will need a small shirt box, red and green scrapbook papers, craft glue, green and red Sensational Strips paper strips, ruler, tape, $3\frac{3}{8}$"w dimensional papier-mâché star, cotton swab, red chalk, linen thread, embellishments for name (we used a round letter tile and sticker, a stamped tag, a sticker adhered to torn cardstock, and a letter cut from a magazine), artificial berries, date stamp, and a black ink pad.

1. Wrapping excess to the inside, cover lid and bottom of box with scrapbook papers; trim excess as needed and glue to secure.

2. Glue green paper strips across lid. Knot centers of several paper strips together. Pull ends of strips over straight edge of ruler to curl; tape strips to lid.

3. Cut a piece of red scrapbook paper $1/4$" smaller than star; glue to star. Use cotton swab to apply chalk to edges of scrapbook paper. Glue a green paper strip around sides of star. Tie a length of thread into a bow around one star point. Glue or adhere embellishments and berries to star. Stamp date on star. For hanger, knot a length of thread $1/2$" from ends; glue knot and ends to top point of star. Tape star hanger to lid.

CARAMEL SAUCE JAR
(shown on page 73)

You will need light green, blue, and white cardstock; glass jar with lid; small and medium circle and snowflake punches; craft glue; iridescent glitter; and a black fine-point permanent marker.

1. For sleeve, cut a piece of light green cardstock to fit around jar plus 1". Cut a piece of blue cardstock $1/8$" smaller on all sides than green cardstock.

2. Referring to photo and using circle punches for snowman, punch snowman and snowflakes from blue cardstock piece; discard punched shapes. Punch additional snowflakes from a scrap of white cardstock.

3. Center and glue blue cardstock on light green cardstock.

4. For snow, cut a 1"w strip of white cardstock the same length as blue cardstock. Tear away one long edge of white cardstock strip. Arrange and glue snow and white snowflakes to sleeve.

5. Apply glue to desired areas on snow, snowflakes, and around snowman; sprinkle with glitter. Allow to dry, then shake off excess glitter.

6. Use marker to draw snowman features and add message. Overlapping edges at back, glue sleeve around jar.

CANDY CONTAINER
(shown on page 73)

You will need blue cardstock; disposable plastic container with a lid; craft glue; iridescent glitter; dimensional foam dots; assorted snowflake stickers and charms; felt snowman sticker; decorative-edged craft scissors; scraps of print scrapbook paper and black and orange cardstock; $3/8$"w green ribbon; black fine-point permanent marker; and a small tag.

1. Cut a piece of blue cardstock to fit on container lid; glue to lid.

2. Apply glue to desired areas on snowman and snowflake stickers; sprinkle with glitter. Allow to dry, then shake off excess glitter.

3. Using foam dots as desired, arrange and adhere stickers and charms on lid.

4. Referring to photo and using craft scissors as desired, cut snowman's hat and features from scraps of cardstock and print paper. Arrange and glue hat and features on snowman. Knot a length of ribbon and glue to snowman.

5. Use marker to write message on tag; glue tag to snowman.

JELLY JARS WITH BAG

(shown on page 74)

You will need a brown gift bag with handles, red handmade paper, brown cardstock, double-sided tape, assorted red and green scrapbook papers, craft glue, five ³/₈" square silver brads, alphabet beads, ¹/₄"w gold and ³/₈"w green striped ribbons, ¹/₈" dia. hole punch, alphabet stickers, black fine-point permanent marker, two glass jars with lids, and two ¹/₂" dia. silver jingle bells.

Bag

1. Remove handles from bag and discard.
2. Tear a piece of handmade paper to fit bag front. Cut a piece of brown cardstock ³/₄" smaller on all sides than bag front; center and tape to handmade paper. Cut squares from scrapbook papers (ours measure approximately 2"). Arrange and tape squares on brown cardstock. Zigzag stitch around edges of cardstock and squares. Glue handmade paper to bag front.

3. Punch holes in corners of brown cardstock; attach brads through holes. Thread alphabet beads onto a length of gold ribbon; notch ribbon ends. Glue beads to bag above one bottom brad.
4. For tag, cut a rectangle from scrapbook paper; round one end. Cut a piece of brown cardstock ¹/₈" smaller than tag; machine sew to tag. Tear a rectangle from scrapbook paper; glue to center of tag. Punch hole at top of tag. Knot a length of gold ribbon through hole; tie ribbon ends into a bow. Attach remaining brad to hole in tag. Adhere stickers to spell "TO" and "FROM"; write names on tag. Glue tag to bag.
5. Thread ends of a length of green striped ribbon through existing holes in bag or punch holes as needed. Knot ribbon ends to secure.

Jars

1. For each jar, cut a circle of brown cardstock to fit jar lid. Cut a piece of scrapbook paper ¹/₂" smaller than jar lid; center and tape to cardstock. Referring to photo, machine sew across circles. Label, then tape circles to jar lid.
2. Knot the center of a length of gold ribbon through one jingle bell hanger. Catching one gold ribbon end in the knot, knot a length of green striped ribbon around jar; knot gold ribbon ends around knot in striped ribbon.

OLIVE JAR

(shown on page 75)

You will need brown, green, and red cardstock; glass jar with lid; red rickrack; craft glue; black fine-point permanent marker; green scrapbook paper; beading needle; fine-gauge craft wire; wire cutters; small red beads; metal "PARTY," "c," and "s" embellishments; and alphabet stickers.

1. For sleeve, tear a strip of brown cardstock to fit around jar plus 1". Cut a length of rickrack the same length as brown cardstock. Center and glue rickrack on cardstock.
2. For label, tear a square of green cardstock. Cut a square of red cardstock ¹/₄" smaller on all sides than green cardstock. Layer and glue pieces together. Draw a wavy line around edge of green cardstock.
3. Cut a square of green scrapbook paper the same size as red cardstock. Thread a needle with a length of wire. Adding beads as you sew, sew metal embellishments to paper. Adhere stickers to paper to spell "citrus" and "Olives." Referring to photo, glue paper to label.
4. Overlapping edges at back, glue sleeve around jar. Glue label to sleeve.

SNACK TUBE

(shown on page 76)

You will need cheese cookies; double-sided tape; green foil paper; white pom-pom wired trim; red, green, and white cardstock; red checked scrapbook paper; Santa, star, and border stickers; alphabet stamp set; black ink pad; and a ¼" dia. hole punch.

1. Stack desired number of cookies. Overlapping ends at back and securing with tape, wrap cookies in foil paper; secure ends with lengths of pom-pom trim.
2. For sleeve, cut a piece of white cardstock and scrapbook paper to fit around stack plus 1". Trim approximately ¾" from each end of paper. Layer and glue pieces together. Overlapping edges at back, tape sleeve around cookie stack.
3. For label, print "Merry Christmas" on green cardstock; cut out. Adhere border stickers to label edges. Tape label to sleeve.
4. Adhere stickers to sleeve.
5. For tag, cut a rectangle from red cardstock; trim corners from one short end. Stamp "Cheese Cookie Snacks" on tag. Adhere stickers to tag. Punch hole in top of tag. Thread one end of pom-pom trim through hole to secure tag to cookie stack.

KITCHEN TOWEL BAG

(shown on page 77)

You will need a kitchen towel; coordinating embroidery floss; colored pencils; black and white photocopy of photograph; green, tan, and off-white cardstock; craft glue; linen thread; red felt; dimensional foam dot; embellishments for message (we used assorted scrapbook papers and cardstock, a letter tile, a tag, stickers, alphabet stamp set, and a black ink pad); small tag; four buttons; and ¼"w coordinating ribbon.

Refer to Embroidery Stitches, page 186, before beginning project.

1. For bag, matching ends and right sides and using floss and a ¼" seam allowance, fold towel in half and sew side edges together with *Running Stitches*; turn right side out. With seam at center back, use floss and work *Running Stitches* across bottom of bag; press bag.
2. Use pencils to add color to photocopy of photograph as desired. Cut a frame from green cardstock to fit around photograph. Glue photograph behind frame. Leaving thread ends free at one bottom corner, sew around frame with linen thread. Cut a small heart from felt. Use foam dot to adhere heart to frame.

3. For label, cut a piece of tan cardstock ¾" larger on all sides than frame. Cut a piece of off-white cardstock ¼" larger on all sides than tan cardstock. Center and machine stitch outer edges of tan cardstock on off-white cardstock. Glue frame to center of label.
4. Referring to photo, use desired embellishments to add message to label.
5. Print "Pecan Pimiento Cheese" on off-white cardstock; cut out and glue to tag. Thread linen thread ends at bottom of frame through hole in tag; knot to secure.
6. Stitching through label and bag, use linen thread to sew buttons to corners of label.
7. Tie a length of ribbon around top of bag.

Knitting Bee Luncheon

LUNCHEON INVITATION

(shown on page 80)

You will need yellow, red, and green cardstock; brown chalk; alphabet stamp set and ink pad; brown fine-point permanent pen; yellow, striped, and plaid scrapbook papers; craft glue; $5/16$" dia. brad; four $3/16$" dia. eyelets and setter; bee stickers; assorted yarns; and $1/8$" dia. hole punch.

1. Photocopy invitation patterns, onto yellow cardstock; cut out for pages 3 and 4. Turn pages over and draw around pages on another yellow sheet; cut out for pages 1 and 2. Tint edges with chalk.
2. Stamp "what:," "when:," and "how:" on the tabs.
3. Draw lines, $1/2$" apart, across page 2. Write party information on lines, asking guests to knit 4 squares to bring to the party.
4. Cut a $3^{1}/4$" x $4^{1}/2$" piece of yellow paper. Cut a $1^{1}/2$" x $4^{1}/2$" piece of striped paper; tear $1/4$" from one long edge. Glue striped paper to right side of yellow paper; round corners. Center and glue yellow paper on page 1. Zigzag stitch around outer edges of papers.
5. Tear a $1^{7}/8$" x $1^{1}/4$" piece from yellow paper; tint edges with chalk, then stamp "JOIN ME" at center. Tear a $2^{1}/4$" x $1^{3}/8$" piece from plaid paper. Layer and glue pieces together; glue to page 1. Add stickers. Stamp "for a" on page 1.
6. Cut two $2^{3}/4$" x $3/4$" strips from green cardstock; clip corners. Glue strips to red cardstock; trim edges. Stamp "knitting bee" and "LUNCHEON" on strips. Attach eyelets to strips; glue to page 1.
7. Knot lengths of yarn around page 1. Stack pages together. Punch a hole in bottom right corner of invitation. Insert brad through hole to secure pages.

For more information about the Warm Up America! Foundation, visit www.warmupamerica.org.

KNITTING BEE LUNCHEON SQUARES

Finished Size: 7" x 9" (18 cm x 23 cm)

Note: Instructions are written for Medium/Worsted Weight yarn with Bulky Weight yarn in braces { }. If only one number is given, it applies to both weights of yarn.

MATERIALS
Medium/Worsted Weight Yarn {Bulky Weight Yarn}: see individual pattern for yardage
Straight knitting needles, 8 (5 mm){11 (8 mm)} **or** size needed for gauge
Yarn needle

GAUGE: 20{14} sts = 4" (10 cm)

SQUARES
50{36} yards/45.5{33} meters

Cast on 35{25} sts.
Row 1: K5, (P5, K5) across.
Row 2: P5, (K5, P5) across.
Rows 3-6: Repeat Rows 1 and 2 twice.
Row 7: P5, (K5, P5) across.
Row 8: K5, (P5, K5) across.
Rows 9-12: Repeat Rows 7 and 8 twice.

Repeat Rows 1-12 for pattern until piece measures approximately 9" (23 cm).

Bind off all sts in pattern.

SEED STITCH
60{40} yards/55{36.5} meters

Cast on 35{25} sts.

Row 1: K1, (P1, K1) across.

Repeat Row 1 for pattern until piece measures approximately 9" (23 cm).

Bind off all sts in pattern.

DOUBLE SEED STITCH
55{40} yards/50.5{36.5} meters

Cast on 35{25} sts.
Row 1: K1, (P1, K1) across.

Rows 2 and 3: P1, (K1, P1) across.
Row 4: K1, (P1, K1) across.

Repeat Rows 1-4 for pattern until piece measures approximately 9" (23 cm).

Bind off all sts in pattern.

GARTER STITCH
63{50} yards/57.5{45.5} meters

Cast on 35{25} sts.

Knit every row for pattern until piece measures approximately 9" (23 cm).

Bind off all sts in **knit**.

Patterns

CLASSIC COCOA & CREAM

Pear Place Card Holders
and Dinner Napkins

Cone-Shaped Stocking

OLDE WORLD RADIANCE

Embellished Candles, Boxed
Pillow, Embellished Throw,
and Fleur-de-lis Ornaments

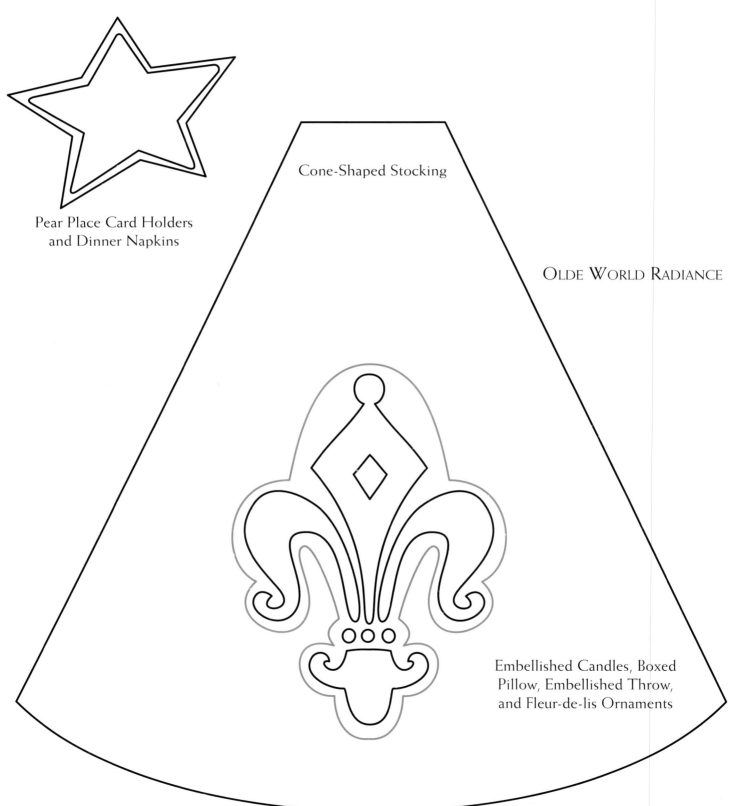

Madonna and Child Painting

Serenity Vase and
Glass Candleholders

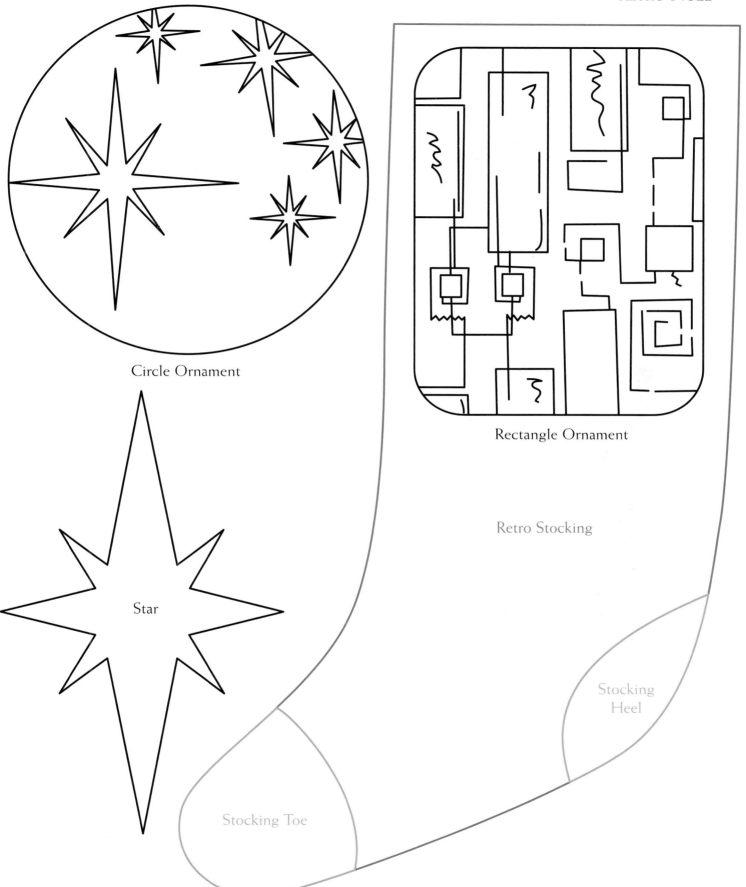

Circle Ornament

Rectangle Ornament

Retro Stocking

Star

Stocking Heel

Stocking Toe

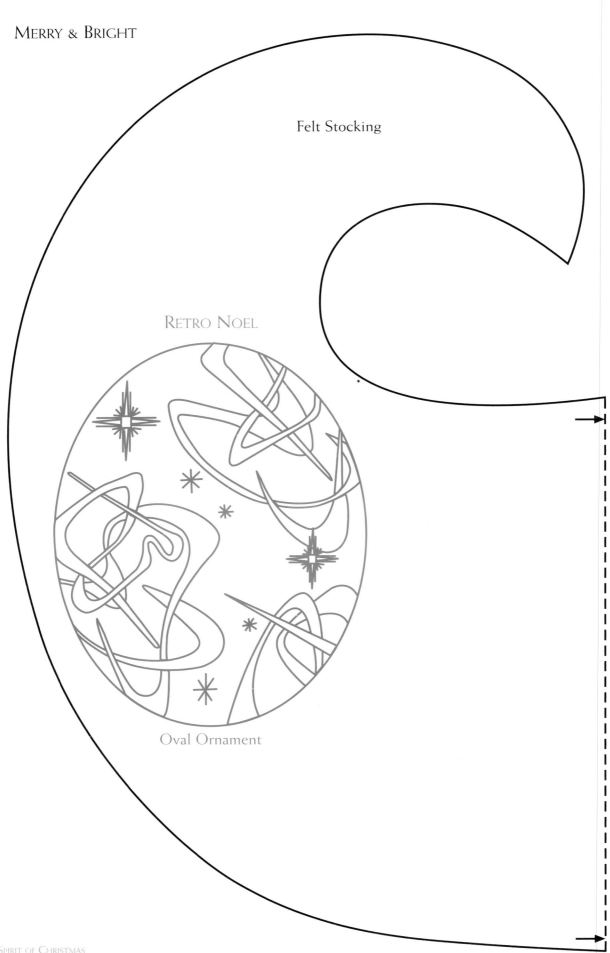

Felt Stocking

RETRO NOEL

Oval Ornament

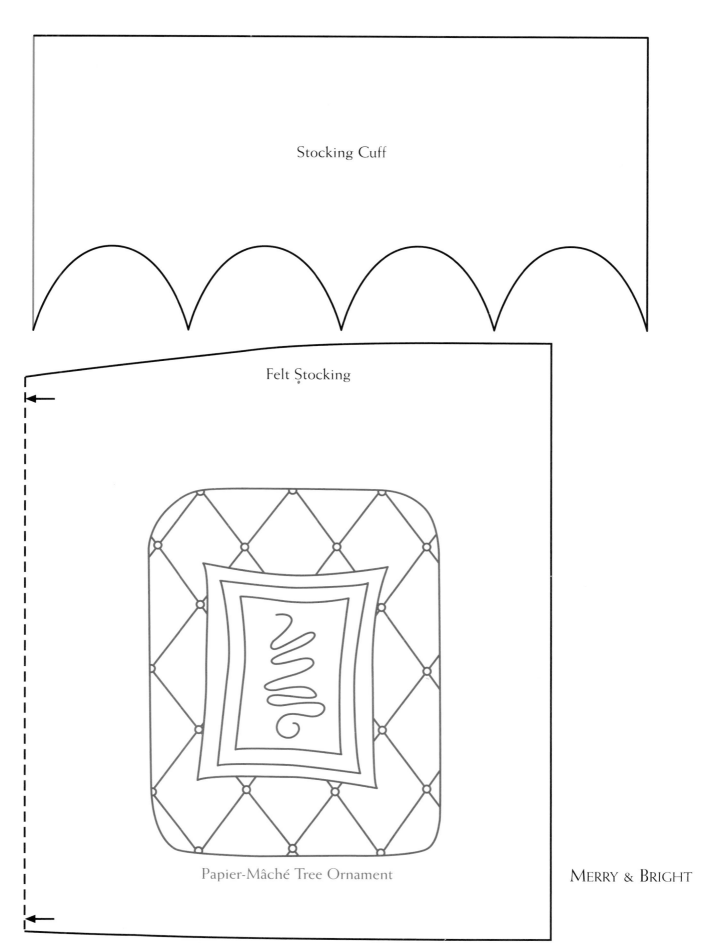

Stocking Cuff

Felt Stocking

Papier-Mâché Tree Ornament

MERRY & BRIGHT

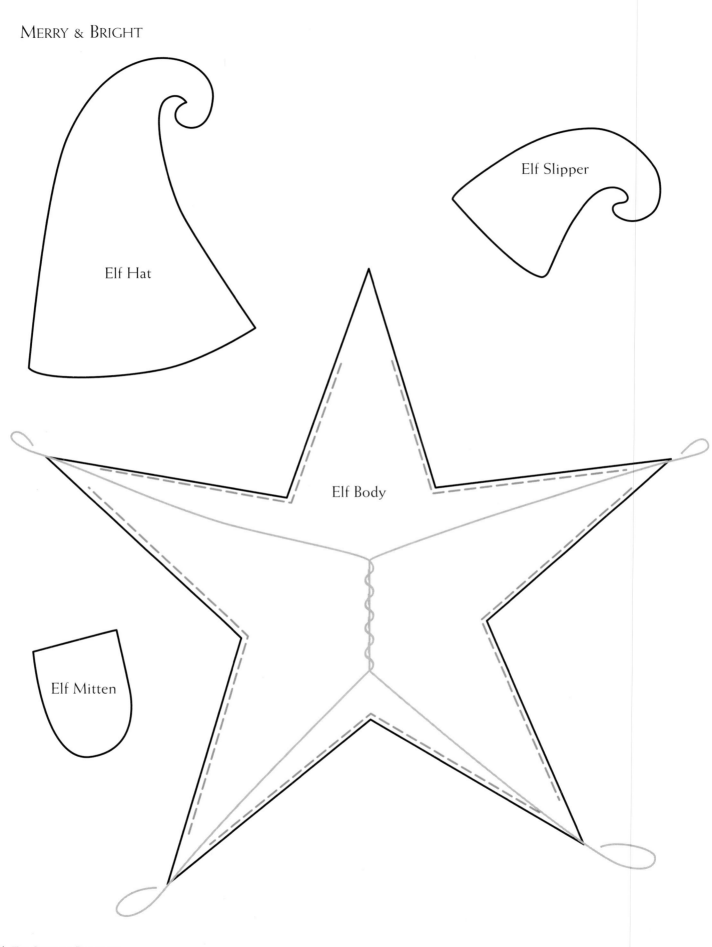

Elf Hat

Elf Slipper

Elf Body

Elf Mitten

Painted Chargers

Flocked Ornament

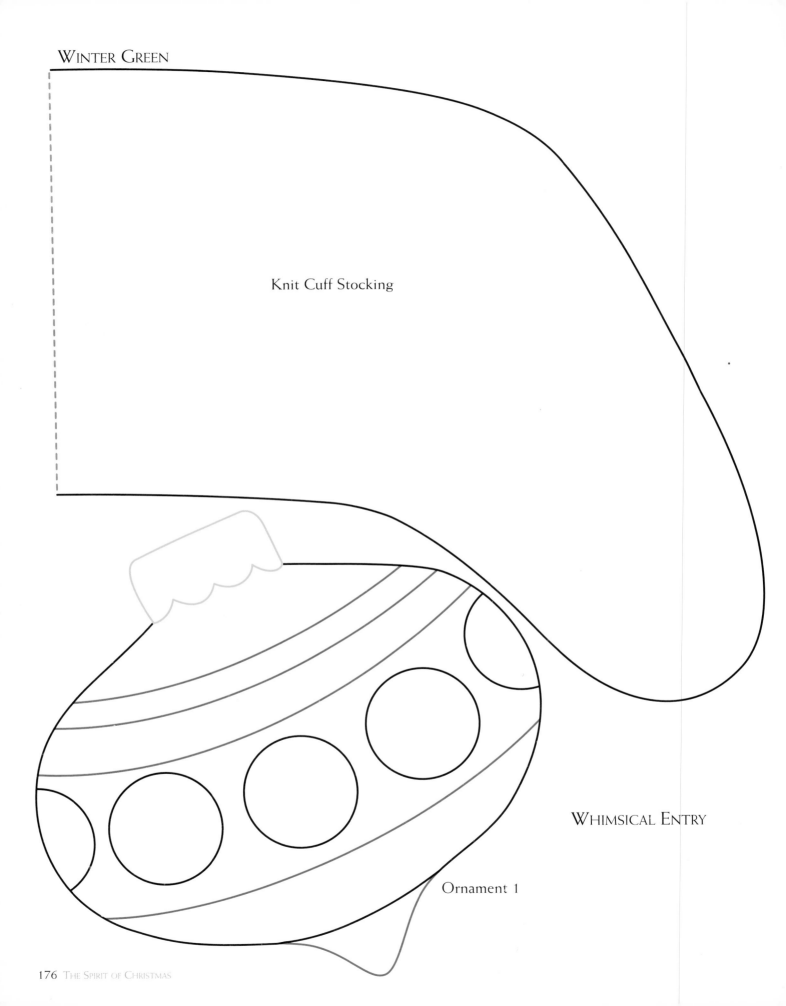

WINTER GREEN

Knit Cuff Stocking

WHIMSICAL ENTRY

Ornament 1

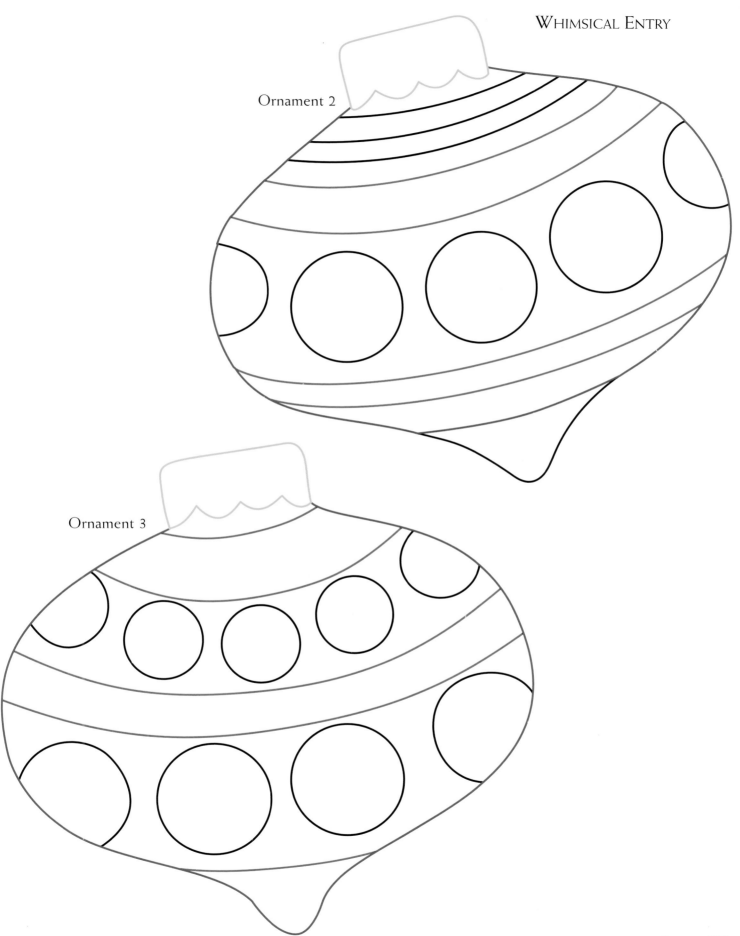

Ornament 2

Ornament 3

Enlarge to 118%.

Man

Enlarge to 130%.

Woman

Use at 100%.

Boy

Santa Box &
Appliquéd Tea Towel

Appliquéd Tea Towel

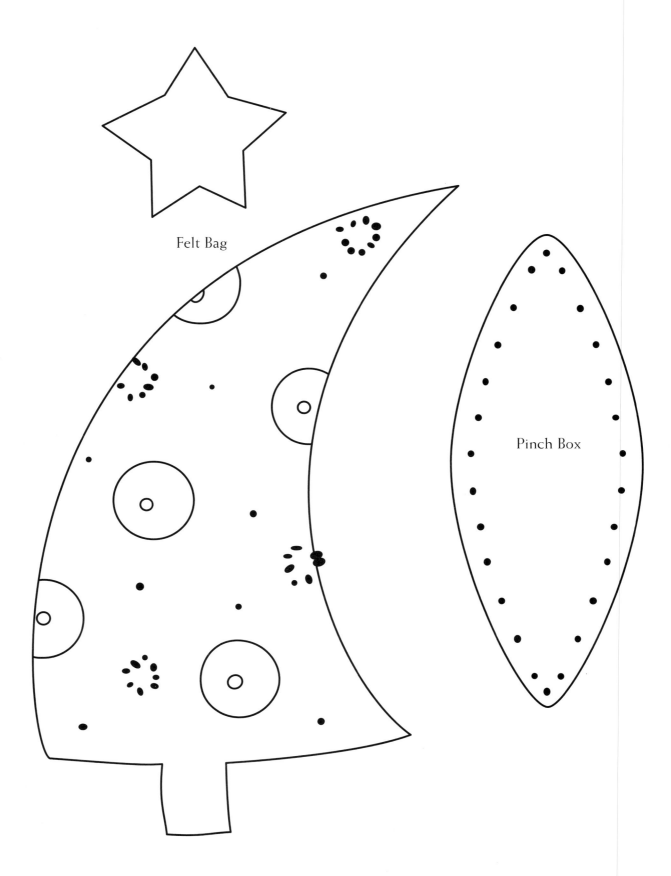

Felt Bag

Pinch Box

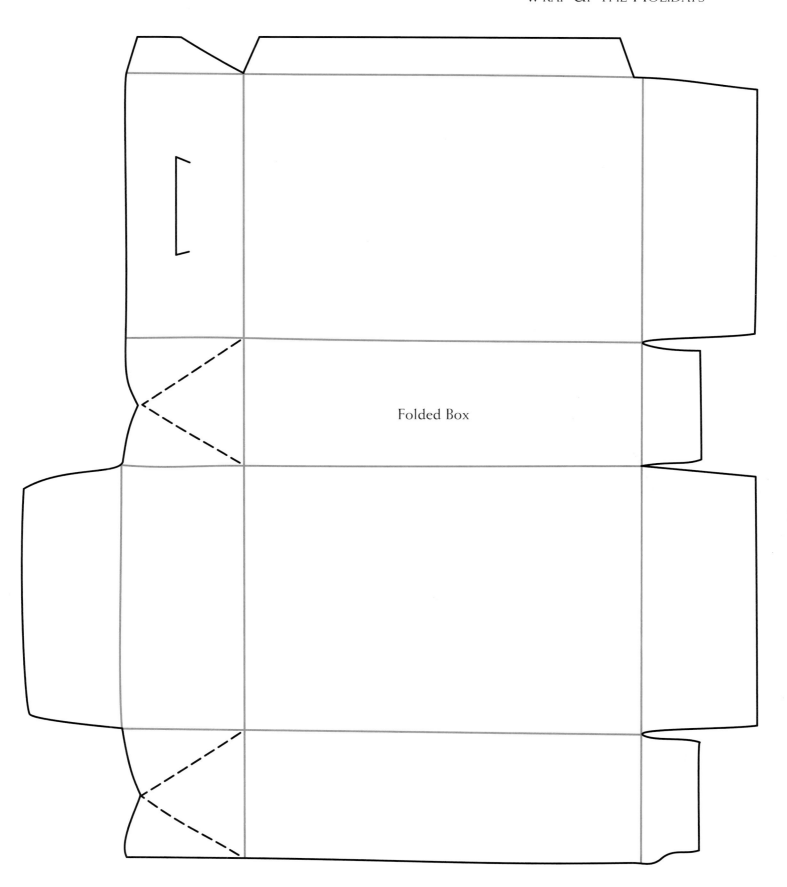

Folded Box

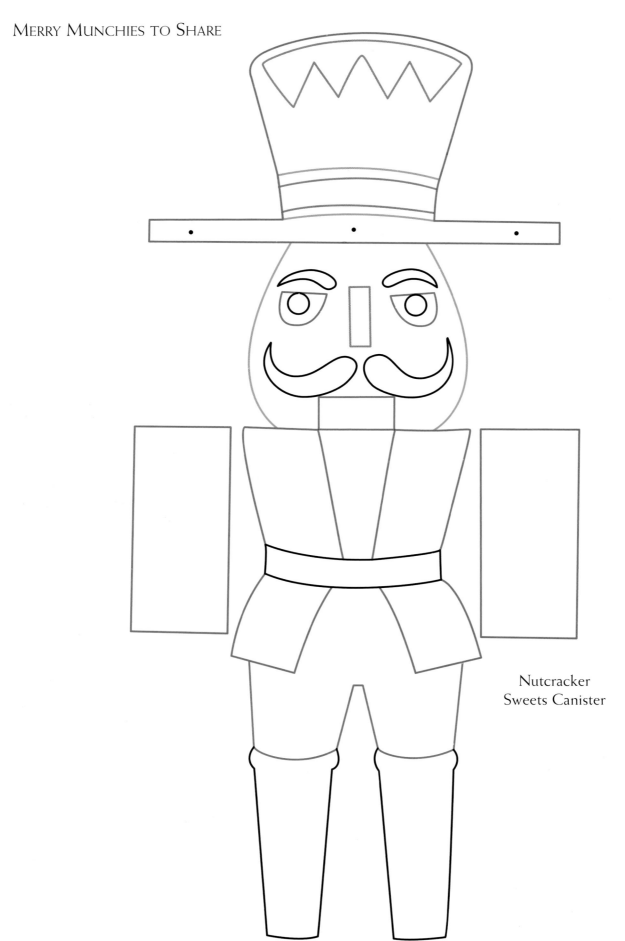

Nutcracker
Sweets Canister

General Instructions

ASSEMBLING ARRANGEMENTS

It is important when assembling decorative arrangements to create a visual balance between the various kinds and sizes of flowers, greenery, and/or decorative items used.

Place tall items at back of arrangement. Arrange focal items, then fill areas between items with medium-size and small items. To add short-stemmed items or small items to a foam-based arrangement, either wrap wire of a wired floral pick around an inconspicuous area of the item or tape or glue pick to the item.

MAKING TASSELS

1. Wrap embroidery floss/yarn around cardboard square.
2. Slide a 4" length of floss/yarn under all strands at one end of square; knot tightly around floss/yarn, then knot ends together to form hanger. Referring to Fig. 1, cut floss/yarn at opposite end of square.

Fig. 1

MAKING PATTERNS

HALF PATTERNS

When only half of a pattern is shown (indicated by a solid blue line on the pattern), fold tracing paper in half. Place the fold along the blue line and trace pattern half; turn folded paper over and draw over traced lines on remaining side of paper to form a whole pattern.

MULTIPLE-PART PATTERNS

When tracing a multiple-part pattern, match the dashed lines and arrows to trace the patterns onto tracing paper, forming a whole pattern.

STACKED OR OVERLAPPED PATTERNS

When pattern pieces are stacked or overlapped, place tracing paper over pattern and follow a single color to trace pattern. Repeat to trace each pattern separately onto tracing paper.

PAINTING TECHNIQUES

PAINTING BASECOATS

A basecoat is a solid color of paint that covers the project's surface.

Use a medium to large paintbrush for large areas and a small brush for small areas. Do not overload brush. Allow paint to dry after each coat.

TRANSFERRING PATTERNS

Note: If transferring pattern onto a dark surface, use a light-colored transfer paper to transfer pattern.

Trace pattern onto tracing paper. Using removable tape, tape tracing paper pattern to project. Place transfer paper (or graphite paper), coated side down, between project and tracing paper. Use a stylus or pencil to lightly draw over pattern lines onto project.

TRANSFERRING DETAIL LINES

To transfer detail lines to project, using removable tape, tape tracing paper pattern to project. Place transfer paper (or graphite paper), coated side down, between project and tracing paper over painted basecoat and use a stylus or pencil to lightly draw over detail lines of pattern onto project.

DETAILS/LINE WORK

To prevent smudging lines or ruining your pen, let painted areas dry before adding details/line work.

Use a permanent marker or paint pen to draw over transferred detail lines or to create freehanded details on project.

If painting, mix paint with water to an ink-like consistency. Dip a liner brush into thinned paint. Use tip of brush to outline or create details on project.

SHADING AND HIGHLIGHTING
(side loading)

Dip one corner of a flat brush in water; blot on a paper towel. Dip dry corner of brush into paint. Stroke brush back and forth on palette until there is a gradual change from paint to water in each brush stroke. Stroke loaded side of brush along detail line on project, pulling brush toward you and turning project if necessary.

For shading, side load brush with a darker color of paint.

For highlighting, side load brush with lighter color of paint.

DOTS

Dip a spouncer, dauber, round paintbrush, the handle end of a paintbrush, or one end of a toothpick in paint and touch to project. Dip item in paint each time for uniform dots.

SPATTER PAINTING

This technique creates a speckled look on the project's surface.

Dip the bristle tips of a dry toothbrush into paint, blot on a paper towel to remove excess, then pull thumb across bristles to spatter paint on project. Repeat until desired effect is achieved. Allow paint to dry.

SEALING

If a project will be handled frequently or used outdoors, we recommend sealing the item with clear sealer. Sealers are available in spray or brush-on forms and in a variety of finishes. Follow the manufacturer's instructions to apply sealer.

Some projects will require two or more coats of sealer. Apply one coat of sealer and allow to dry. Lightly sand with fine-grit sandpaper, then wipe with a tack cloth before applying the next coat.

MAKING APPLIQUÉS

To prevent darker fabrics from showing through, white or light-colored appliqué fabrics may need to be lined with fusible interfacing before applying paper-backed fusible web.

To make reverse appliqué pieces, trace pattern onto tracing paper; turn traced pattern over and continue to follow all steps using the reversed pattern.

1. Use a pencil to trace pattern or draw around reversed pattern onto paper side of web as many times as indicated for a single fabric. Repeat for additional patterns and fabrics.
2. Follow manufacturer's instructions to fuse traced patterns to wrong side of fabrics. Do not remove paper backing.
3. Cut out appliqué pieces along traced lines. Remove paper backing.
4. Arrange appliqués, web side down, on project, overlapping as necessary. Appliqués can be temporarily held in place by touching appliqués with tip of iron. If appliqués are not in desired position, lift and reposition.
5. Fuse appliqués in place.

MAKING A FABRIC CIRCLE

1. Cut a square of fabric the size indicated in project instructions.
2. Matching right sides, fold fabric square in half from top to bottom and again from left to right.
3. Tie one end of string to a pencil or fabric marking pen. Measuring from pencil, insert a thumbtack through string at length indicated in project instructions. Insert thumbtack through folded corner of fabric. Holding tack in place and keeping string taut, mark cutting line (Fig. 1).

Fig. 1

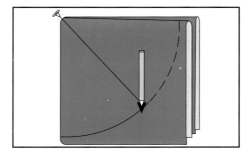

4. Cut along drawn line through all fabric layers.

EMBROIDERY STITCHES
FRENCH KNOT

Bring needle up at 1. Wrap thread once around needle and insert needle at 2, holding thread with non-stitching fingers (Fig. 1). Tighten knot as close to fabric as possible while pulling needle back through fabric.

Fig. 1

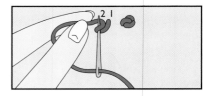

RUNNING STITCH

Referring to Fig. 2, make a series of straight stitches with stitch length equal to the space between stitches.

Fig. 2

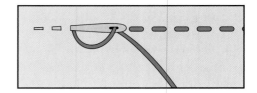

WELTING

1. Measure the raw edges of project. Add 5" and cut a piece of cord that length. Cut a bias strip of welting fabric the length of the cut cord and wide enough to wrap around the cord plus 1" (this strip may be pieced if necessary).
2. Center cord on wrong side of bias strip. Matching long edges, fold bias strip over cord. Using zipper foot and gently stretching fabric as you sew, baste next to cord.

3. Beginning at center bottom, pin welting to right side of project, clipping seam allowance to fit. Starting 1" from one end of welting, baste welting to project front, stopping about 2" from other end. Leaving needle in fabric, cut off welting so ends overlap by 1". Remove 1" of basting from each end of welting. Holding the fabric away from cord, trim cord ends to meet exactly. Insert one end of welting fabric into the other; turn top end under ½" and baste in place (Fig. 1).

Fig. 1

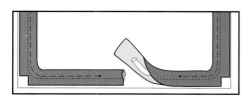

KNIT AND CROCHET BASICS

ch(s)	chain(s)
cm	centimeters
K	knit
mm	millimeters
sc	single crochet(s)
st(s)	stitch(es)
tog	together
YO	yarn over

★ — work instructions following ★ as many **more** times as indicated in addition to the first time.
( ) or [ ] — work enclosed instructions as many times as specified by the number immediately following **or** work all enclosed instructions in the stitch or space indicated **or** contains explanatory remarks.
colon (:) — the number(s) given after a colon at the end of a row or round denote(s) the number of stitches you should have on that row or round.

KNIT 2 TOGETHER
(abbreviated K2 tog)
Insert the right needle into the front of the first two stitches on the left needle as if to knit *(Fig. 1)*, then knit them together as if they were one stitch.

Fig. 1

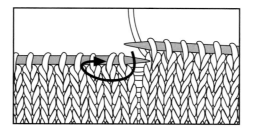

YARN OVER
Bring the yarn forward between the needles, then back over the top of the right hand needle, so that it is now in position to knit the next stitch *(Fig. 2)*.

Fig. 2

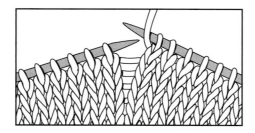

CROCHET TERMINOLOGY	
UNITED STATES	**INTERNATIONAL**
slip stitch (slip st) =	single crochet (sc)
single crochet (sc) =	double crochet (dc)
half double crochet (hdc) =	half treble crochet (htr)
double crochet (dc) =	treble crochet (tr)
treble crochet (tr) =	double treble crochet (dtr)
double treble crochet (dtr) =	triple treble crochet (ttr)
triple treble crochet (tr tr) =	quadruple treble crochet (qtr)
skip =	miss

KNITTING NEEDLES		
UNITED STATES	**ENGLISH U.K.**	**METRIC (mm)**
0	13	2
1	12	2.25
2	11	2.75
3	10	3.25
4	9	3.5
5	8	3.75
6	7	4
7	6	4.5
8	5	5
9	4	5.5
10	3	6
10½	2	6.5
11	1	8
13	00	9
15	000	10
17	---	12.75

ALUMINUM CROCHET HOOKS	
UNITED STATES	**METRIC (mm)**
B-1	2.25
C-2	2.75
D-3	3.25
E-4	3.5
F-5	3.75
G-6	4
H-8	5
I-9	5.5
J-10	6
K-10½	6.5
N	9
P	10
Q	15

Yarn Weight Symbol & Names	SUPER FINE 1	FINE 2	LIGHT 3	MEDIUM 4	BULKY 5	SUPER BULKY 6
Type of Yarns in Category	Sock, Fingering Baby	Sport, Baby	DK, Light Worsted	Worsted, Afghan, Aran	Chunky, Craft, Rug	Bulky, Roving
Knit Gauge Ranges in Stockinette St to 4" (10 cm)	27-32 sts	23-26 sts	21-24 sts	16-20 sts	12-15 sts	6-11 sts
Advised Needle Size Range	1-3	3-5	5-7	7-9	9-11	11 and larger

Project Index

Recipe Index

Credits

We want to extend a warm thank you to the generous people who allowed us to photograph our projects at their homes.

- *Classic Cocoa & Cream and Yuletide Fiesta:* Doug and Leighton Weeks
- *Olde World Radiance:* Shirley Held
- *Retro Noel and Resplendent in Red:* Amy Williams
- *Merry & Bright, Winter Green, and Knitting Bee Luncheon:* Scott and Angela Simon
- *Blue & Bronze Entryway:* Carol Jeffrey
- *Dickens Entry:* Dan and Jeanne Spencer
- *Whimsical Entry:* Kathy Holt
- *Neighborhood Round Robin:* Alda and Buddy Ellis

Our sincere appreciation goes to Jerry Davis Photography, Jason Masters of Nola Studio, Mark Mathews Photography, Larry Pennington of Pennington Studios, and Ken West Photography, all of Little Rock, Arkansas, for their excellent photography. Photography stylists Sondra Harrison Daniel, Janna B. Laughlin, Christy Myers, and Jan Nobles also deserve a special mention for the high quality of their collaboration with these photographers.

We would like to recognize Royal Langnickel for the paintbrushes used on all painted designs and National Nonwovens for providing the wool felt used in this book. And our thanks go to Husqvarna Viking Sewing Machine Company of Cleveland, Ohio, for providing the sewing machines used to make many of our projects, and to Midwest of Cannon Falls for props in some of the photographs. For the many fine yarns used to create our knit and crochet projects, we thank Caron International, Coats & Clark, Lion Brand Yarns, and Spinrite companies.

We are sincerely grateful to Liz Field for sharing her technical expertise, to Suzie Puckett for the timely editorial copy, and to Rose Glass Klein for testing some of the recipes in this book.